FLEAS, FL[IES AND]
FRIARS

Nicholas Orme

FLEAS, FLIES, AND FRIARS

Children's Poetry from the Middle Ages

Nicholas Orme

First Published 2011
by Impress Books Ltd

Innovation Centre, Rennes Drive, University of Exeter Campus,
Exeter EX4 4RN

© Nicholas Orme 2011

Typeset in Joanna by Swales & Willis Ltd, Exeter, Devon
Printed and bound in England by imprintdigital.net

British Library Cataloguing in Publication Data
A catalogue record for this book is available from the British Library

ISBN 13: 978–1–907–60523–9 (paperback)
ISBN 13: 978–1–907–60528–4 (ebook)

CONTENTS

FOR ALISON AND MIKE

CHILDREN'S POETRY FROM THE MIDDLE AGES

Ever since there was speech, there must have been verse, rhythmic or rhyming, and children who heard, sang, or spoke it. Two thousand years ago, Jesus pictured them calling to one another in the market place,

> We piped to you, and you did not dance;
> We mourned, and you did not cry.[1]

But for a long time, the verse that children knew and spoke went unrecorded, except for rare allusions like that of Jesus. In classical times and for most of the Middle Ages, the majority of writings were concerned with other things: at least those writings that we

---

1 Matthew, 11.16–17; Luke, 7.32.

now possess. Only very gradually did adults, and later children themselves, begin to note down the verses and songs of childhood, and little even of what they noted exists today.

The earliest surviving poetry for children in medieval Britain comes from the grammar schools: schools that taught Latin to boys and youths. From Roman times, pupils in these schools studied Latin literature in verse, one of the most popular texts being a collection of wise sayings from the third century AD, known as the *Distichs of Cato*. Such poetry was adult in origin, but may be called children's literature since it was read by children. In about 1200, textbooks of grammar for schools (which had previously been written in Latin prose) began to be produced in Latin verse as well. It seems odd today to write a textbook in verse, but when copies of books were few, parts of such texts could be committed to memory as a substitute for a written version. For the rest of the Middle Ages, down to about the 1520s, verse textbooks were commonly used in grammar schools, and excerpts from two of them are included in this anthology.

Soon after 1200, the writing of textbooks in verse spread to other subjects than Latin grammar. Courtesy books appeared, meaning poems that taught good manners, chiefly aimed at boys of the higher classes of society. These poems gave advice on how to behave at the table or when speaking to other people, and were produced first in Latin and later also in English. In the 1240s, an English knight named Walter of Bibbesworth wrote a treatise in verse for children learning French, and in the fifteenth century some writers in English compiled works in poetic form to teach morality and wisdom to teenagers, including a Scottish gentleman named Rait. By that time, there was also a handbook in rhyme about hunting, ostensibly by a gentle-woman for her son but doubtless meant for any young men of the gentry.

Most of the verse of medieval children, however, existed only in speech. There were many short rhymes: nursery rhymes, tongue-twisters, riddles, charms, game rhymes, and insults, as well as adult songs that children heard and sang. Stories were told as ballads to gatherings of adults where children might be present: stories like the adventures of Robin Hood. Nearly all this oral verse has been lost and it took a long time for anyone to write down the words. One thirteenth-century Latin sermon refers to a children's game rhyme in English, and another to an English song sung by a teenage girl about a search of a boy friend. But it is only after 1400 that more than a few scraps of such verse survive, and their survival reflects an important change in technology: the advent of paper.

Paper was cheaper than the parchment that had hitherto been available for writing permanent records, and more durable than the wax or wooden tablets used for jotting down temporary ones. In grammar schools in particular, paper enabled boys and youths to keep notes of their work, and several collections of their notes survive from the fifteenth and early sixteenth centuries. Such collections need not have contained any children's verse, but fifteenth-century schoolmasters did not forbid, and perhaps even encouraged, their pupils to write down bits of poetry from time to time as a challenge to translate it into Latin. They probably thought that this would keep their class amused during the grind of school lessons. As a result of this, school notebooks provide us with fragments of verse and a few longer pieces that children (or more accurately teenagers) invented themselves or recorded from what they were saying and hearing: precious survivals of the oral culture of the day.

The fifteenth century is also notable in producing narrative literature that children could enjoy. Previously, although children were probably often listeners while literature was read aloud by adults, such literature was primarily written for adults. After 1400, there is a stronger sense that stories were being composed or recycled in a way that was suitable for both adults and children, or even for children alone. The Robin Hood ballads come into this category, as do some romances, and there is a comic tale in verse called *The Friar and the Boy* which appears to have been chiefly aimed at children. By 1476, when William Caxton began to print books in England, children were sufficiently important as readers for his opening list of titles to include four short works in verse especially

3

for them. All four were instructive in nature, notably an English translation of the well-known courtesy poem *Stans Puer ad Mensam*, but later on Caxton and his successors like Wynkyn de Worde also published stories suitable for young people.

The result of these developments is that a wide variety of poems and verses can be collected that were written up to about 1500 and have some connection with children. Some were composed or copied by young people themselves, others by adults for them to use. This poetry has not received much notice from scholars of literature in Britain, because it is scattered and fragmentary, and there are many larger and more ambitious works for adults that merit attention. In 1978, however, Professor Helen Cooper produced a notable pioneering anthology called *Great Grandmother Goose*, which brought together a modernised collection of scraps of English verse from the later Middle Ages. These scraps are roughly of the kind that we associate with the term 'nursery rhymes': tiny stories, short lyrics, bits of fantasy, and satirical or proverbial couplets.

This is an admirable collection for general readers to learn about medieval culture. A problem with it is that many of the pieces cannot be definitely linked to children. For example, Professor Cooper included three of the famous 'Rawlinson lyrics' written down on a single parchment leaf in the early fourteenth century. These lyrics, 'Maiden in the moor lay', 'The Irish dancer', and 'Stand all still', could equally well be adult songs aimed principally at adults. We have no knowledge of when they were sung or to whom. Children may have listened to them and enjoyed them, but we cannot be sure.

My own anthology of late medieval children's literature has been drawn up on two different principles. First, it centres on verses that can be shown to have been composed, copied, used by, or aimed at children or teenagers, whether by adults or children themselves. There are some exceptions to this. Chaucer's 'Prioress's Tale' and John Trevisa's reminiscences of his school days were not written expressly for children. Nor were the accounts of children's games by Rait and Alexander Barclay. They have been

4

included because they illustrate aspects of childhood that cannot easily be depicted from poems produced for children or by them. The vast majority of the items that I have collected, however, have some provable link with children, using that word to include adolescents in their teens.

Secondly, the range of poems has been extended from short scraps to include relevant passages from longer poems and, in one section, to print three fairly lengthy stories in verse of the kind that children are likely to have heard round about 1500. I have also taken material from works that circulated in England in Latin and French as well as in English. My anthology is arranged in five sections. The first two focus on the short lyrical pieces and scraps, together with some excerpts from treatises in verse that deal with childhood or were written for children. The third section presents a group of works for young people on behaviour, the fourth contains the three long stories, and the fifth brings together verse materials that relate to school life, including translations from Latin grammars and poems read in classrooms.

The anthology is aimed first and foremost at general readers, not at scholars who would require a very different kind of work. I would like to make such readers aware that literature in verse for children existed, and still exists, from the later Middle Ages. To reach the general reader, I have had to recast the material. I have translated such of it as was written in Latin and French, and I have modernised the English, Middle English as it is technically known, in a more understandable way. I have occasionally abridged works to make them more concise, or to emphasise certain sections, the abridgements being indicated with dots.

Inevitably, such treatment modifies not only the words but the character of the poems as they were written, but that is the price that has to be paid for making them accessible. To minimise the change, I have kept as close as I could to the original metres and rhyme-schemes as well as retaining some obsolete words that help to preserve the flavour of the original texts, with explanations in footnotes. Once or twice I have rewritten freely, where a passage would otherwise be incomprehensible or inappropriate. Notes at the end of the book explain where each extract can be found in its original version, usually in a scholarly edition.

I hope, dear reader, that you will gain from this selection an idea of the poetry written for children, or said and sung by them, at the very beginning of the history of children's literature in Britain. Through the poetry, you will also learn more about how medieval children grew up, and be able to see beyond the popular perception that they were small adults, living through brief and impoverished childhoods. A medieval childhood could indeed be cut short by disease or distressed by poverty, but while children were alive they shared in a rich culture of songs, sayings, rudenesses, riddles, tales, and (at the higher levels of society) works of instruction as well.

GROWING UP

In the 1240s, Walter of Bibbesworth, a knight of Essex, wrote a pioneering work in the history of childhood. His *Treatise* on the French language was compiled in verse for a lady of the gentry named Denise de Montchesney to help her teach it to her children: in verse so that it could be learnt by heart and remembered. Walter's work drew on a growing interest among the scholars of his day in how children were formed and developed, physically and mentally. Accordingly, he started his work with short accounts of birth, babyhood, dressing, and food. As these were meant for children to hear and read, they count as children's literature as well as being scenes of childhood drawn by an adult.

The circulation of Walter's book was largely confined to the gentry, but all children came into contact with songs and rhymes of one kind or another. Only one true lullaby survives that was sung to children, but there are several verses that resemble nursery rhymes: not identical with the classic nursery rhymes of later centuries, but similar in nature. Adults also sang their own songs to children. A character in William Wager's Tudor play, *The Longer*

Thou Livest, tells how he learnt twenty or more of them while sitting on the lap of his mother's servant woman, and some of these are included in the following section. Other verses survive which show how children absorbed the sounds and activities of everyday life. Each of these was recorded in a school exercise book, showing that it was something that a child or teenager remembered and wished to write down.

As children ceased to be toddlers and became more active and sociable, they played games and sports. In only one case do we possess a medieval rhyme associated with a game, which appears at the beginning of the section on Words, Rhymes, and Songs, but there are two good descriptions in verse of young people's recreations. The first occurs in a fifteenth-century treatise by another lay writer from among the gentry, a Scot named Rait. He wrote the work to teach his son wisdom about human affairs, shaping his advice around the seven ages of man and the different characteristics of each one. The second comes from Alexander Barclay's early sixteenth-century *Eclogues*, and is a perceptive account of how the games of children altered with the seasons of the year.

The cycle of the year was also important to children because of its religious festivals. Shrove Tuesday, the last day before Lent, was a day when boys took cockerels to school to fight them, and there is a Latin poem about such a fight. St Nicholas Day, 6 December, and Holy Innocents Day (or Childermas), 28 December, were other special days when a boy-bishop led the services in church. Christmas was a time of jollification for all, and some Christmas carols explicitly mention the presence of the young as well as the old, two of which are included in this section. They remind us that children, then as now, were not restricted to their own social activities; they joined in many adult ones, and eagerly so.

BABIES AND TODDLERS

Walter of Bibbesworth began his book to teach children French with an account of babies. This helped him to get his pupils' attention, because children are interested in birth and babyhood, and enabled him to introduce them to words in French relating to the subject:

When a woman's time is near
That her infant will appear,
Let her find a midwife, wise
To assist her and advise.
When the child is born at last,
Tie it up with swathings fast,[1]
In a cradle lay it softly
With a nurse to rock it oftly.

Babies first may only crawl
For they cannot walk at all,
And they dribble quite a bit,
Making messes on their kit,
So the nurse, the clothes to spare,
Should provide a bib to wear.

When they start to walk, beware!
Dirts and hurts are everywhere,
So, for safety, please employ
A small servant girl or boy
To attend them and ensure
That they don't fall on the floor.

Walter does not mention another common custom: putting food by the head of a sleeping child to deflect or confuse evil spirits. This was roundly condemned by the writer Robert Mannyng soon after 1300, but only in terms of the belief, not the practice!

The food that you lay at the child's head,
For evil spirits, were better laid.
If you let it for them lie,

---

1 Babies were swaddled: closely wrapped around with strips of linen.

9

It is a wicked heresy.
Lay it for love of the Holy Ghost,
Father, and Son, one God steadfast!

LULLABIES

The first songs that medieval children heard were lullabies or, as they were known, 'cradle songs'. Mothers and nurses were visu-alised as 'lulling' children to sleep by singing the syllables 'la, la'. Several lullabies survive in medieval manuscripts, but they are all pieces of adult religious literature picturing the Virgin Mary singing to the Baby Jesus about their family's poverty, or his coming life and death, like this one:

This yonder night I saw a sight,
A star as bright as any day,
And ever among a maiden sang
'By, by, lully, lullay'.

This maiden was Mary, she was full mild,
She kneeled before her own dear child;
She lulled, she lapped,
She turned, she wrapped,
She wept and wept away,
She turned him, she dressed him,
She soothed him, she blessed him,
She sang 'dear son, lullay'.

In fact, the only description of real mothers singing lullabies, in a fourteenth-century sermon, says that they sang 'old songs'. The one quoted has nothing in it about children; instead it is a lyric warning a girl against a naughty young man:

Watch well, Annot,
Thy maiden bower,
And get thee from Walter,
For he is lecher!

FOOD AND CLOTHES

After describing birth and babyhood, Walter of Bibbesworth reminded children about how they should dress themselves, and taught them the French words for their clothes:

> Put your clothes on; don't refuse
> Breeches, gloves, and also shoes;
> Hat on head for rain or sun;
> Buttons – do up every one.
> Put your belt around your waist,
> Then make sure the end is placed
> Through the buckle till the pin
> Holds the belt-end safely in.

He also talked about suitable food for small children: bread, eggs, and apples:

> If your toddler feels unfed
> And should point towards the bread,
> Give it then a decent bit,
> Less if you are short of it.
> Eggs at dinner time are good,
> If it likes that kind of food.
> To remove the shell is right,
> And the lining and the white,
> But the yolk is good to eat
> And will make a tasty treat,
> Though the germ we all should shun,
> Which is bad for everyone.
> Apples I must mention too,
> And instruct you what to do;
> Everyone likes apples well,
> Children too, as all can tell.
> Take the stalks off, pare the skin,
> Then to eat you may begin;

Throw away the apple core,
But plant the pips to grow some more.

NURSERY RHYMES

There is no reason to doubt that medieval adults interacted with children and sang or spoke them rhymes like the 'nursery rhymes' of later centuries. This one looks like a rhyme for a child because it is repetitive and talks of a 'little pretty boy':

I have twelve oxen, and they be fair and brown,
And they go a-grazing down by the town,
   With hey, with ho, with hoy!
Sawest thou not mine oxen, thou pretty little boy?

I have twelve oxen, and they be fair and white,
And they go a-grazing down by the dyke,
   With hey, with ho, with hoy!
Sawest thou not mine oxen, thou pretty little boy?

I have twelve oxen, and they be fair and black,
And they go a-grazing down by the lake,
   With hey, with ho, with hoy!
Sawest thou not mine oxen, thou pretty little boy?

I have twelve oxen, and they be fair and red,
And they go a-grazing down by the mead,
   With hey, with ho, with hoy!
Sawest thou not mine oxen, thou pretty little boy?

This is an example of the 'catastrophic accident' in one short verse, familiar in later rhymes like 'Jack and Jill' and 'Humpty Dumpty':

Tom-a-lin and his wife and his wife's mother,
They went over a bridge all three together.
The bridge was broken and they fell in;
'The devil go with all', said Tom-a-lin.

These are imaginative rhymes, picturing animals and insects as human beings

> The hare went to market, scarlet for to sell;
> The greyhound stood before him, money for to tell.
>
> Hares and foxes, mice and rats,
> Prayed to reremice,[1] flies, and gnats
> That they should arm them with old mats
> To feeze[2] out of town hounds and cats.

And this is a similar rhyme with three verses, unless it is a collection of three different rhymes:

> The cricket and the grasshopper went out to fight,
> With helmet and haburgeon[3] all ready dight.[4]
> The flea bore the banner as a doughty knight,
> The beetle trumpeted with all his might.
>
> The hare sat upon the hill and fastened her shoon,[5]
> And swore by the buttons that were thereupon
> That she would not rise nor go on
> Till she saw twenty hounds and one.
>
> The miller sat upon the hill,
> And all the hens of the town drew him till;
> The miller said, 'Shoo, hen, shoo;
> I may not shake my bag for you.'

While this rhyme is rather mysterious: proverb, charm, or very likely a counting-out rhyme?

> The owl to the stone and the stone to the owl,
> But ever abideth the silly[6] owl.

---

1 Bats. 2 Drive. 3 Mail shirt. 4 Dressed. 5 Shoes. 6 Originally meaning poor, pitiable.

SONGS MY MOTHER TAUGHT ME

William Wager's play, The Longer Thou Livest, the More Fool
Thou Art, *was published in 1569. In it the Fool quotes from
eight songs which he says that he heard from 'a fond [i.e. foolish]
woman to my mother. As I was wont in her lap to sit, she taught
me these and many other'. Although the source dates from after
the end of the Middle Ages, the songs appear to be traditional.
One is* Tom-a-lin, *mentioned above, but most of the rest seem to
be songs of adults. They are included here because they remind
us that children learn adult songs or overhear them being sung,
and may remember them for the rest of their lives:*

> The gentle broom on hive hill,
> Broom, broom, on hive hill,
> The gentle broom on hive hill,
> The broom stands on hive hill.

> Robin, lend to me thy bow, thy bow;
> Robin, the bow; Robin, lend to me thy bow.

> There was a maid came out of Kent,
>   Dainty love, dainty love,
> There was a maid came out of Kent,
>   Dangerous be.
> There was a maid came out of Kent,
> Fair, proper, small, and gent,[1]
> As ever upon the ground went,
>   For so should it be.

> Come over the burn, Bessie,
>   My little pretty Bessie,
> Come over the burn, Bessie, to me.

> The white dove sat on the castle wall;
> I bend my bow and shoot her I shall;
> I put her in my glove, both feathers and all.

---

1 Gentle, perhaps in the sense of belonging to the gentry.

*And the Fool uses the time-honoured adult way of ending a
session of singing or talking to children:*

> I laid my bridle upon the shelf;
> If you want any more, sing it yourself.

SOUNDS OF EVERYDAY LIFE

*We grow up hearing sounds, and some of the verses recorded in
school exercise books describe what children heard in everyday
life. There is the tame bird in the bird-cage:*

> At my house I have a jay,
> He can make many a lay:[1]
> He can bark as a fox,
> He can low as an ox,
> He can hiss as a goose,
> He can bray as an ass,
> He can croak as a frog,
> He can bark as a dog,
> He can chatter as a wren,
> He can chatter as a hen,
> He can neigh as a steed,
> Such a bird is mad indeed.

'The swallow twittering from the straw-built shed':

> If I were as swift as a swallow,
> Many good morsels I would swallow;
> Beyond the crescent[2] I would fly,
> So that no other bird should me follow.

The travelling fishmonger shouting his wares:

> Five herrings for a penny, blood in the gill,[3]
> Six for another – pill, garlic, pill![4]

---

1 Song. 2 The moon. 3 Herrings look like that when they are fresh. 4 And
pull some garlic to eat with them.

15

A sing-song down at the village inn:

> We are three; let us sing;
> A three-part song is just the thing.
> Who sings my song
> And who tells my tale,
> Let him pay for the ale.

And the clacking wheel of the village mill, whose cogs drive the millstones as the miller's daughter looks on. Or is this verse quite what it seems? Mills were notorious places for philandering: remember Chaucer's Reeve's Tale!

> The miller's daughter knows well
> How many cogs run in the wheel:
> One cog and a cog, both cogs well.

AN UNUSUAL CHILDHOOD

Some of the most detailed accounts of childhood in medieval literature relate to Jesus. They originated in the early Middle Ages and are entirely imaginary, but they include many descriptions of the play, schooling, and work of a child and teenager, all with supernatural happenings. Here is one of the stories, from a version in medieval English verse:

> It happened on a certain day
> That all the children had the will
> To travel in a grand array
> Down to the well, their pots[1] to fill.
> Each was resolved to make no stay;
> All would the first and quickest be,
> So each one hurried on his way
> To reach the well more speedily.
> Jesus to fill his pot began,

---

1 Pitchers or jars.

But Archa thought some harm to do:
He broke the pot, the water ran;
'Yours', Jesus said, 'will shatter too.'

But, see! the pot displays no break,
And Jesus turning to his friends,
Says 'Now, let's play beside the lake,
And hang our pots upon the ends
Of sunbeams', so they do, and his
Hangs up, but all the others fall
And smash – oh, what a misery this,
And Archa sobs the most of all!
'Now, see', says Jesus, 'who's at fault.
You broke my pot, the water ran;
From what you suffer here, be taught
"Wrong earns the ills that it began".'

Then Joseph, who was present there,
Said 'Jesus has great mastery
Of power, as we are aware
From all the wonders that we see
On every day, on every hand.
My pot, now broken into three,
May be restored, if you command,
So help us, Jesus, lovingly'.
'Joseph', says Jesus, 'for your sake,
The pots shall now be whole and strong';
They are, and all the children take
Them homewards with a joyful song.

GAMES AND HOLIDAYS

Rait's account of the seven ages of man defined childhood as the second age, lasting from three till seven. He took the view of philosophers that this age was dominated by children's wish to play:

The second age, so I am told,
Extends from three to seven years old,
When children have a wish alway
With flowers for to jape and play,
With sticks and also splinters small
To build up chamber, spence,[1] and hall,
To make a white horse of a stick,
Of broken bread a sailing ship,
Of ragwort stems a burly spear,
And of a sedge a sword of war,
A comely lady from a clout,[2]
And be right busy thereabout
To dress it prettily with flowers,
And love these puppet paramours.

In the third age, from eight to fifteen, children moved on to more active or intellectual games:

Now at the mark[3] and other while
They run at bars[4] and at the ball,
And at catch they play withal;
Now at the tables,[5] now at the chess
Well oft, but seldom at the mass,[6]
And much at playing at the dice,
A pastime I hold most unwise.

Alexander Barclay, writing in the early sixteenth century, noticed how boys varied their games and activities according to the time of year. Then, as now, football loomed large, although its season opened later than nowadays: when bladders became available in November!

---

1 Buttery: store where drink was kept and served.   2 Piece of cloth.
3 Probably with archery in mind.   4 The running game of prisoner's bars.
5 Backgammon.   6 i.e. attending church.

Each time and season hath his delight and joys:
Look in the streets, behold the little boys,
How in fruit season for joy they sing and hop;
In Lent is each one full busy with his top;[1]
And now in winter, for all the grievous cold,
All rent and ragged a man may them behold;
They have great pleasure, supposing well to dine,
When men be busied in killing of fat swine;[2]
They get the bladder and blow it great and thin,
With many beans or peasen[3] put within.
It rattleth, soundeth, and shineth clear and fair
While it is thrown and cast up in the air;
Each one contendeth and hath a great delight
With foot and with hand the bladder for to smite . . .
Running and leaping they drive away the cold.

Barclay does not include cock-fighting in his list, but it was a common activity of boys on Shrove Tuesday. This fifteenth-century Latin poem, from a school note-book, praises the achievements of Cob, the winning bird, which belonged to a boy named Chelyng:

Cockerel denominated
'Cob', with feathers decorated,
Coloured yellow overall,
At his beak the birds defenceless
Flee in terror like the senseless,
With a clamour horrible.

Wings outstretched at every comer,
Like a peacock in the summer,
Every feather gleaming bright,
Legs like posts ensure survival,

---

1 Whipping tops in Lent may have symbolised the whipping of Christ on Good Friday.   2 This was in November.   3 Peas

Pressing hard on every rival;
He is victor in the fight.

With a body as unyielding
As a stone set in a building,
Never will he choose to flee;
And the boys declare directly
That by custom and correctly,
Chelyng gets the victory.

Shrove Tuesday was also Pancake Day: a day to celebrate (if you were a schoolboy) with a verse of Latin puns:

Liba libens libo; post liba libencius ibo.
Pancakes I gladly will taste, and after more gladly make haste.

But a complaint in a fifteenth-century school exercise book from Wiltshire reads:

I have not eaten half my fill of pancakes and of fritters, and therefore no thanks to our cook who should have prepared enough, having flour and lard enough ready with him in the kitchen!

Two other great days of the year for boys were the festivals of St Nicholas and the Holy Innocents on 6 and 28 December. On one or both of these days, churches chose a boy bishop to lead the services, and other boys took part or attended. Here is part of the Latin 'sequence' for 6 December which they might have sung or listened to. Nicholas was the patron saint of children: believed to have fasted even at his mother's breast and later to have been a hard-working student. Through one of his miracles after death, he was also the patron of sailors:

Let us now rejoice together,
With the common voice of all,

Praising Nicholas the Blessed
On his solemn festival;
Who while even in the cradle
Kept the Church's fasting days,
And his mother's milk refusing,
Merited the highest praise;
Growing then to study learning,
Diligent as he could be,
Both immune and utter stranger
To the world's depravity . . . .

Certain sailors onward wending,
With the raging floods contending,
And their vessel almost broken,
In their peril all are crying,
Each one fearing he is dying,
And a single prayer is spoken:
'Nicholas, do not forsake us!
Safely to a harbour take us,
To our dread of death be woken!
Save our ship, to harbour lead it,
You, whose help to those who need it,
Of your sanctity is token!'

As they clamour in their durance,
Comes a voice of reassurance,
'I will help you; I am here!'
All at once the tempest lessens,
Waves subside into quiescence;
Calm and order reappear . . . .

For us in this world abiding
Through a sea of vices sliding,
Shipwreck is our sorry story;
Holy Nicholas, still hear us,
To the harbour safely steer us
Where is always peace and glory . . . .

So let those now celebrating,
Round the world rejoicing send,
And may Christ, a crown donating,
Greet us when our lives shall end.

*After the morning services were over on 6 and 28 December,
groups of boys toured the neighbourhood, singing and collect-
ing food or money, before sitting down to a feast. But few feasts
can have equalled that of the choristers of York Minster in 1396,
which cost:*

For bread, 7*d*. For lord's bread, 4*d*. For ale, 21*d*. For veal and mut-
ton, 9½*d*. For salt, 4*d*. For two ducks, 4*d*. For twelve hens, 2*s*. 6*d*.
For eight woodcocks and one plover, 2*s*. 2*d*. For three dozen and
ten fieldfares, 19*d*. For small birds, 3*d*. For wine, 2*s*. 3*d*. For diverse
spices, 11*d*. For sixty warden-pears, 5½*d*. For honey, 2½*d*. For
mustard, 1*d*. For two pounds of candles, 2½*d*. For flour, 2*d*. For
firewood, 1½*d*. Also, to the cook, 6*d*. Total, 15*s*. 6½*d*.

*Finally, there was Christmas. This, in a large household, would
include communal jollifications, with everyone expected to con-
tribute something. Here is a carol (carols were originally songs
with a chorus, not necessarily religious) that might have been
sung at the beginning of the fun. Each person, large or small, must
play a part, including grooms (adult male servants), pages (boy
servants), and the marshal himself: the master of ceremonies:*

Make we merry, both more and less,[1]
For now is the time of Christmas!

Let no man come into this hall,
Groom, page, nor yet marshal,
But that some sport he bring withal,
For now is the time of Christmas!

---

1 Both the greater and the lesser of us.

22

If that he say he cannot sing,
Some other sport then let him bring,
That it may please at this feasting,
   For now is the time of Christmas!

If he say he can naught do,
Then for my love ask him no moe,[1]
But to the stocks then let him go,
   For now is the time of Christmas!

*At some point, one or more carols in praise of Christmas would
certainly be sung. The one that follows, by the fifteenth-century
poet James Ryman, expressly mentions that children are in the
audience:*

Both man and child, have mind of this:
   How God's own Son of bliss,
Of Mary mild a man now is,
   To die for man's amiss.[2]

The King of bliss his Father is,
   And Jesus is his name,
To bring mankind to heaven's bliss
   For which he bears our blame

And in a stall this child was born,
   Between both ox and ass,
To save us when we were forlorn
   Of grace, as his will was.

When he was born, that heavenly King,
   Of Mary, queen of bliss,
Then *Gloria* did the angels sing
   Deo in excelsis . . . .

---

1 More.   2 Sin.

Now laud we God of heaven's bliss
  With heart and will and mind,
Who, of a maiden, man now is,
  To bliss to bring mankind.

And at a manor house, when the performers left the hall at the end of the evening, they would remember to pray for the lord and lady and their children:

We pray for the lord of all this hall,
And for the lady, that fair it her fall!
And for the children, both great and small,
That God keep every one,
For they have given us each good cheer,
So pray for them now, all you who are near,
That to heaven they shall go from here,
When their joy on earth is done.

WORDS, RHYMES, AND SONGS

Most of the poetry in the previous section was composed by adults for children, or about children's activities. We shall now encounter more verses that were invented by children or teenagers themselves, or were adopted by them from songs and sayings of adults. A major source of the rhymes in the following section is the school exercise books of the period after 1400. Those that we possess were probably written by teenagers or young adults, because they are well presented and were worth keeping, but they show their writers to have been in contact with verse that looks more childish in character.

The exercise books, together with some evidence from elsewhere, reveal that children knew and used a wide range of rhymes. They shouted abuse in verse. They gabbled tongue-twisters, asked riddles, and said charms or curses. At least one running game involved chanting a formula before and afterwards. And there were nonsense rhymes, which developed out of the nursery rhymes told to children when they were tiny. Even older children liked to imagine animals doing human tasks, or in topsy-turvy situations.

Were these rhymes known only in specific places at certain times, or did they circulate widely and for long periods? It is difficult to be sure in most cases, because the sources available to us are limited. Some rhymes may have been made up by one person for one occasion. 'I saw a sparrow', 'At harvest time', or 'Underneath a louver' may all have come from grammar-school classrooms as challenges for turning into Latin.

Others, however, must have been widely known. 'A fox and a polecat' and 'Hairy Scot' are both found in more than one text, while the rhyme about Martin Swart appears to have been composed in about 1487 but was still in use eighty years later. In addition, the same types of rhymes recur in different times and places, so that there was probably a national culture of rhyming. Amusing verses, or songs about current events, were likely to spread across the nation fairly quickly, just as such verses do in modern times.

Childhood faces two ways, both inwardly to its own interests and outwardly to the adult world around. There are traces of the adult world in the rhymes. Medieval children were as aware of sex as modern ones, perhaps more so. School exercises often dealt quite frankly with this in prose, and some children may have known rhymes like that of the seduced maiden. They certainly knew about love and marriage, and sang or said rhymes about them of the kind that are printed at the end of this section.

Children were also in touch with rougher and crueller adult behaviour and humour. We have already met with a poem in praise of cock-fighting. In the following section you will find a warning against cursing fellow-children or animals, as well as rude remarks about friars, ale-sellers, shoemakers, and Scots. Later on, we shall encounter violent episodes in the ballad of Robin Hood and the story of Sir Aldingar, as well as beatings (promised or delivered) in *The Friar and the Boy* and in the section on School Days. Medieval society was crueller than ours in the sense that it officially sanctioned corporal and capital punishment, and sometimes tolerated cruelty to animals. Children grew up in this society and the rhymes and stories they liked were bound to reflect it.

AN EARLY OBSERVER

In 1389, the scholar John Trevisa, translating into English the thirteenth-century Latin encyclopaedia On the Properties of Things, *wrote:*

Children are soft of flesh, lithe and pliant of body, able and light in moving, clever to learn carols. . . . They love play and games and vanities. . . . They love talkings and counsels of such children as they are, and forsake and avoid the company of older people. . . . Suddenly they laugh and suddenly they weep. Always they cry and jangle and jape and make faces.

A GAME RHYME

One of the oldest recorded verses of children is a game rhyme. It occurs in a Latin sermon of the thirteenth century, whose author compares those who promise to lead good lives and fail to do so, with children playing the game 'How many miles to Beverley-ham?' This was a chasing game between two or more children. It started with a dialogue:

First child: How many miles to Beverleyham?
Second child: Eight, eight, and other eight.
First child: May I come there by daylight?
Second child: Yes, by God, if your horse be light.

Then, says the preacher, 'the first speaker begins a good run, as fast as he wishes to go, and then dances back and is in his original place and says:

27

Ha! Ha! petty pace,[1]
Yet I am where I was.'

In other words, he has successfully run across a space without being caught and returned safely to his home base. A later version of the same rhyme is 'How many miles to Babylon?'

TONGUE-TWISTERS

Both of these turn up in manuscripts made by school pupils during the fifteenth century. Versions of the first have been found in recent times:

Three grey greedy geese
Flew o'er three green greasy furrows;
The geese was grey and greedy,
The furrows green and greasy.

This one includes a swipe at friars, who were seen as scroungers for charity and competitors with other clergy:

Fleas, flies, and friars – foul fall them these fifteen years!
For none that is here loveth fleas nor flies nor friars.

RIDDLES

Riddles were popular and the one that follows occurs in two or three school exercise books in English or Latin, once with seven men. But what is the answer?

Three headless men played at the ball;
One handless man served them all;

---

1 Slowcoach.

One mouthless man stood and laughed
As a cripple dragged his cloak.

This too may be a riddle, unless it is a bit of a ghost story:

Bloodless and boneless standeth behind the door!

One poem is a whole collection of riddles. It is first found in the notebook of a schoolboy from Devon in the fifteenth century, but later turns up widely in England and Scotland in different versions:

Will you hear a wondrous thing
Betwixt a maid and the foul fiend?

Thus spoke the fiend to the maid:
   'Believe on me, maid, today.
Maid, may I thy lover be?
   Wisdom I will teach thee. . . .

'What is higher than is the tree?
   What is deeper than is the sea?
What is sharper than is the thorn?
   What is louder than is the horn?
What is longer than is the way?
   What is redder than is the day?
What is better than is the bread?
   What is sharper than being dead?
What is greener than is the wood?
   What is sweeter than is the note?
What is swifter than is the wind?
   What is richer than is the king?
What is yellower than is the wax?
   What is softer than is the flax?'

The maid prays to Jesus for inspiration and protection. Then she says:

'Heaven is higher than is the tree;
   Hell is deeper than is the sea;

Hunger is sharper than is the thorn;
   Thunder is louder than is the horn;
Looking is longer than is the way;
   Sin is redder than is the day;
God's flesh[1] is better than is the bread;
   Pain is stronger[2] than being dead;
Grass is greener than is the wood;
   Love is sweeter than is the note;
Thought is swifter than is the wind;
   Jesus is richer than is the king;
Sapphire is yellower than is the wax;
   Silk is softer than is the flax.
Now, thou fiend, still thou be!
Will I speak no more with thee!'

At which the devil instantly disappears, as devils do when you recognise and name them!

CHARMS AND CURSES

Children said charms to heal and protect themselves. When you were stung by a nettle, you put a dock leaf on the place and said

In dock, out nettle.

This was for saying before you went to bed:

Mark, Matthew, Luke, and John,
The bed be blest that I lie on.

And this was a curse if, despite the blessing prayer, you were troubled by a nightmare, 'the witch's daughter':

---

1 The consecrated wafer in church.   2 The word is 'sharper' in the devil's question.

If it so betide
The witch's daughter over thee ride,
Both shall have God's curse:
The witch's daughter and hers.

While this was a warning to thieves, written by the same fifteenth-century schoolboy in Devon in his schoolbook:

Who steals this book should be hanged by the neck;
Who blames what's here may kiss my rear.

But a writer of the same century warned children not to cast spells on other children or on animals, which apparently involved turning round, either clockwise or anti-clockwise, while the spell was said:

By street or way if thou shalt go,
From these two things restrain thee, though:
Neither to harm child nor beast
With casting, turning west or east.

NONSENSE

Children loved nonsense verse long before Edward Lear or Lewis Carroll wrote it. This verse comes from a school exercise book in English, along with a Latin translation. It is fixated on the rhymes for 'sparrow':

I saw a sparrow
Shoot an arrow
By a harrow
Into a barrow.

While the composer of this was fascinated by the rhymes for 'clatter':

At harvest time carts do clatter;
Paddocks[1] crowd that sit by the water;

---

1 Frogs.

31

Whoso falls in the fen, besmirches his hat;
Whoso may not see, he stumbles the rather;
And he that hath an evil wife, he thriveth the later.

This rhyme occurs only in Latin, but one can work back towards the original English from which the student was translating:

I saw three snails
Joining their tails
When the dawn was breaking,
    And the cockerel crew
    And the foxes blew,
At the church's dedicating.

And this is a nonsense carol. The whetstone (a stone for sharpening tools) was associated with lying, so it is the prize for the best liar:

Hey, hey, hey, hey,
I will have the whetstone if I may.

I saw a dog cooking sowse,[1]
And an ape thatching a house,
And a pudding eating a mouse:
    I will have the whetstone if I may.

I saw an urchin[2] shape[3] and sew,
And another bake and brew,
Scour the pots as they were new:
    I will have the whetstone if I may.

I saw a codfish corn sow,
And a worm a whistle blow,
And a pie[4] treading[5] a crow:
    I will have the whetstone if I may.

---

1 Pickled pork.   2 Hedgehog.   3 Cut out a garment.   4 Magpie.   5 Mating with.

I saw a stockfish drawing a harrow,
And another driving a barrow,
And a saltfish shooting an arrow:
    I will have the whetstone if I may.

I saw a boar burdens bind,
And a frog wool-skeins wind,
And a toad mustard grind:
    I will have the whetstone if I may.

I saw a sow her kerchiefs[1] wash,
The second sow had a hedge to plash;[2]
The third sow went to the barn to thresh:
    I will have the whetstone if I may.

I saw an egg eating a pie;
Give me drink, my mouth is dry;
It is not long since I told a lie:
    I will have the whetstone if I may.

RUDE REMARKS

Children have always loved insulting each other, and some of their insults get into exercise books. The first may be a playground chant, sung when somebody had a sticky bur or goose-grass fixed to their clothes.

Hur! Hur!
The shrew[3] bears the bur!

The next may be a simple insult, or a reply to one:

John, John, pick a bone;
Tomorrow thou shalt pick none.

The third is based on the idea 'I have something nice, and you have something nasty'.

---

1 Head-dress.   2 Plait together.   3 Villain.

33

> I will have the whip and you will have the pip;[1]
> I will have a rose and you will have a snotty nose.

Schoolmasters even let boys write down insults in their exercise books and translate them into Latin. All three of the previous rhymes were recorded in this way, and the next few insults (in prose not verse) are found in a published collection of Latin school exercises from the beginning of the sixteenth century:

> Thou stinkest.
> Thou art a false knave.
> Thou art worthy to be hanged.
> His nose is like a shoeing horn.
> Turd in thy teeth!
> I shall kill thee with my own knife!

UNPOPULAR PEOPLE

Children grew up in a world of social tensions. They learnt that their elders disliked certain kinds of people. As well as friars, these included haywards who rounded up stray animals, and tapsters or ale-sellers who were often believed to sell poor-quality drink. All these feature in this rhyme alongside a fox and a polecat – animals that stink:

> A fox and a polecat,
> A friar and a hayward,
>   Standing in a row,
> A tapster standing by their side,
> The best of the company is an old shrew.

The next rhyme features souters, meaning cobblers or shoemakers, also as stinkers, perhaps because they sometimes used dung to treat shoe leather:

---

1 Respiratory disease of poultry.

Souters have an extravagant pride,
For they will ever on paniers ride,
    Like poulterers on pokes.[1]
Where in land we may them find
We shall turn their arse against the wind,
For they stink like dogs.

In times of political turmoil, young people took sides and sang the songs that their elders made on the subject. Henry 'Hotspur' Percy, who rebelled against Henry IV and was killed at the battle of Shrewsbury in 1403, was remembered much later:

Harry Hotspurs hath a halt
    And he is fallen lame;
Francis Physician for that fault
    Swears he was not to blame.

In 1423, a Scottish battalion was mauled while fighting with the French against the English at the battle of Verneuil in France. An exultant song was made about this, which found its way into a school exercise book from Lincolnshire soon afterwards. The phases when the moon was crooked (or new) and when it was waning were unlucky times:

Hairy Scot in a raveling,[2]
Wast thou at Verneuil at the wrestling?
In the crook of the moon went thou thitherward,
And in the wild waning came thou homeward,
There wast thou thrown in the midst of the place,
And thy neck broke thee through thy evil grace.

And in 1487 a song was made about the battle of Stoke in which Henry VII defeated the pretender Lambert Simnel and his German

---

1 Bags. 2 Skin boot with the hair on the outside.

mercenaries, led by one Martin Schwarz. A chorus from the song
is mentioned being sung to a child eighty years later:

> Martin Swart and his man, sodledum, sodledum,
> Martin Swart and his man, sodledum bell.

LOVE, SEX, AND MARRIAGE

*Love and marriage are frequent topics in medieval literature for
children and teenagers. This reflects the interest of children in the
doings of their elders and the more practical desire of teenagers
to find partners. Here boys are shown anxiously trying to press
their suits with girls:*

> Underneath a louver[1]
> Plucked I a plover;
> Go to Joan Glover
> And say that I love her
> By the light of the moon;
> See that it be so done.
>
> Flowers in my arbour, they grow green;
> Unless my lady love me well, my dog will die for spleen.

*Girls are portrayed as being just as eager to find suitable men to
get married:*

> At stone-throwing my lover I chose,
> And at wrestling I did him lose.
> Alas! that he so quickly fell:
> Why stood he not better, vile gorel?[2]

---

1 The smoke-hole in the roof of a hall without a chimney.   2 Low, fat fellow.

O Robin, I will marry you
Underneath a woodland bough,
With a ring made of a rush,
Because that will be good enough.

Wed me, Robin, and bring me home;
Have I aught, have I naught, then I am a dame.[1]

And inevitably there were seductions, prompting songs that may have been partly meant as warnings to teenage maidens but also slyly aimed to be entertaining:

Alas! alas! the while;
Thought I of no guile,
    So have I good chance.
Alas! alas! the while
    That ever I could dance.

I led the dance on Midsummer Day;
I made small trippings, truly to say;
Jack, our holy-water clerk,[2] came by the way,
And looked upon me – he thought to be gay.[3]
    Thought I of no guile.

Jack, our holy-water clerk, the young stripling,
For the choosing of me he came to the ring,[4]
And he tripped on my toe and made a twinkling;
Ever he came near; he spared for no thing.
    Thought I of no guile.

Jack, you know, pleaded in my fair face;
He thought me full worthy, so have I God's grace;

---

1 A married woman.   2 A teenage lad who assisted the parish priest.   3 Smart
or lively.   4 Girls dancing in a ring.

37

As we turned our dance in a narrow place
Jack gave me his mouth; a kissing there was.
    Thought I of no guile.

With the sad sequel . . .

The other day at prime[1] I came home, as I ween;[2]
Met I my mother, peevish and keen,
'See, thou strong strumpet, where hast thou been?
Thy tripping and thy dancing, well it will be seen!'
    Thought I of no guile.

Ever by and by she reached me a clout;
Ever I bore it privately while that I might,
Till my girdle arose, my womb grew out;
Ill-spun yarn, ever it will out;
    Thought I of no guile.

---

1 Dawn or soon after.   2 As I think.

MANNERS MAKETH MAN

Every society has standards of how to behave, both rationally (ethics) and in practice (good manners). These are generally learnt and passed around in speech and by example, but during the Middle Ages it became the fashion to write them down, especially rules about manners, so that children and young people could learn them formally.

These writings are known as 'courtesy books'. The earliest ones were compiled in western Europe during the twelfth century and were aimed at clergy. By the thirteenth century, they were also being written for children: at first in Latin, later in English, and often in verse so that they could be easily remembered. One of the most popular in England was the Latin poem *Stans Puer ad Mensam*, 'the boy standing at the table', by Robert Grosseteste, bishop of Lincoln from 1235 to 1253. He specialised in bringing up noble boys as pages in his household, and his work tells such boys how to behave when they are serving at a lord's table, eating at table by themselves, or relating to other people at other times.

When Grosseteste was asked how he had become such an expert on courtesy, given that he came from fairly humble origins, he said that he had lived in spirit in the courts of King David and King Solomon, who were greater kings even than the king of England. In other words, he had learnt such things from the Bible, in which the books of Proverbs, Ecclesiastes, and Ecclesiasticus in particular contain a good deal of advice about behaviour.

Stans Puer ad Mensam was widely read in medieval grammar schools. In the fifteenth century, it was translated into English by John Lydgate and other versions of it were made with additional material. These translations, like the original poem, were usually aimed at boys. Much less advice was produced for girls, but three poems survive from the fourteenth and fifteenth centuries that were meant for them, of which *The Good Wife Taught her Daughter* is included below.

Alongside these indoor books of advice, there grew up a parallel body of literature which gave advice about hunting. This was the chief outdoor recreation of the male nobility and gentry, and occasionally of their wives and daughters as well. Hunting became a very mannered sport. Its followers were expected to use the proper words for animals and groups of animals, blow the right horn signals, and carve up the carcasses they captured in the correct way. These procedures and others are described in a fifteenth-century work in verse called *Tristram*, which claims to have been written by a mother for her son, so that it also falls within the scope of poetry for young people.

BEHAVIOUR FOR BOYS

Children, especially boys, were constantly reminded of the importance of behaving properly. Many proverbs were quoted on the subject, and simple verses like these:

> Rax and wax,[1]
> Thrive and thee,[2]
> And good man be.

---

1 Stretch and grow. 2 Prosper.

When thou art in Rome,
Do so of their doom;[1]
When thou art elsewhere,
Do as they do there.

When I lent, I had a friend,
And when I asked he was unkind;
Thus of my friend I made my foe,
And therefore will I lend no more.

In the fifteenth century, someone produced a longer piece of guidance to be memorised. It might be called the 'Advisable Adverbs':

Arise early,
Serve God devoutly,
The world busily,[2]
Go your way steadfastly,
Answer politely,
Go to eat hungrily,
And get up temperately,
And go to supper soberly,
And to your bed merrily,
And be there cheerfully,
And sleep securely.

As already mentioned, there were also long poems about behaviour, especially for boys. The most popular of these, Stans Puer ad Mensam *by Robert Grosseteste, was translated into English by John Lydgate, monk of Bury St Edmunds, who died in about 1451. The translation circulated widely and was one of the first works to be published by William Caxton when he starting printing in England in 1476:*

My dearest child, I want you to be able
To grow up virtuously, at any price,

---

1 Judgment.   2 One of many anticipations of the so-called 'Protestant ethic'.

So when you stand beside your master's table,
Behave, while you are young, by my advice
And set your heart on learning to be nice.
First, when you speak, be careful what you say,
And do not fidget either, by the way.

Do not keep looking round, don't be engrossed
In all the bustle of your master's hall.
Don't slouch and lean your back against a post,
Or look, as in a mirror, at the wall.
Picking your nose is nasty for us all;
Your master wants you quiet and alert,
Not scratching some imaginary hurt.

When people speak to you in any place,
Do not be lumpish, hanging your head down,
But calmly look the speaker in the face,
And walk sedately when you visit Town
To show you are a wise man, not a clown.
Of raucous laughter, too, you should beware,
Particularly when your master's there.

Trim all your nails; make sure your hands are washed
Before you start to eat and when you rise.
Sit down exactly where you have been placed;
To try to bag the best seat is not wise.
Nor, till the course is set before your eyes,
In eating of the bread be over-speedy,
Or everyone will think you very greedy.

Don't grin or make a face while eating food,
Or cry out loudly; silence makes more sense.
To cram your cheeks is also very rude,
And speaking through a mouthful gives offence.
Drink not too quickly or with negligence,
Keep clean your lips from fat of flesh or fish,
And wipe your spoon; don't leave it in the dish.

With soup, do not use bread to sop it up,
Or suck it loudly – that is to transgress,
Or put your dirty mouth to a clean cup,
Or pass drinks while your hands are in a mess,
Or stain your napkin out of carelessness.
Also, beware at meals of causing strife,
And do not make a tooth-pick of your knife.

Put honest mirth into your conversation;
Do not swear oaths, and speak no ribaldry,
And take this proverb for safe preservation:
Do not grab all before you, selfishly;
Share with your fellow, that is courtesy.
Don't load up the left-overs on your plate,
And dirty nails, I pray, eradicate.

In courtesy again, do not emit
Unpleasant noises; they are an offence;
Nor, with old escapades, your fellow twit.
Be mindful of your master; that shows sense.
Don't play with knives; please heed my arguments;
Sit still and decorously when you eat,
And as I said, stop tapping with your feet!

Do not drop sauce or soup upon your chest,
Bring dirty knives into the dining hall,
Or take great overflowing spoonfuls, lest
They slither off; that will not do at all.
Be ready, quick, meek, and dependable,
Awaiting gladly the command to do
Anything that your master orders you.

Again, whenever you shall dine or sup,
Take, like a gentleman, salt with your knife,
And watch that you do not blow on your cup.
Reverence your fellows, and beware of strife;

Seek peace, when in your power, all through your life,
And do not interrupt – it will offend –
Another's tale until the very end.

Don't wag your finger when you tell a tale;
Be careful, as you should when you are young
To drink in moderation wine and ale,
And do not weary people with your tongue.
Facial expressions, when you are among
Your friends, should not be nasty or too nice;
Try something in between is my advice.

Be meek not hasty, and be tractable;
It is worth no one's while to over-reach.
Children, by nature, aren't implacable;
Each is soon roused, but each soon pardons each,
For children's anger, so the sages teach
In ancient books, is only transient;
Give them an apple, and they're soon content.

The wars of children are part fight, part game,
Their quarrels do not breed great violence,
Now play, now weeping, never quite the same,
So when they cry, don't give them audience,
But take your rod and mend their insolence.
In children's hearts no rancour may abide;
When rods are spared, virtue is put aside.

Go, little poem, bare of eloquence,
And pray young children that shall see and read,
That though you do not teach omniscience,
Of all your clauses they should take good heed,
And come from youth to virtue by your lead.
I have not put my name to what I've taught,
But anything that's wrong is Lydgate's fault.

RELIGION

During the fifteenth century, a follower of John Lydgate wrote another version of Stans Puer ad Mensam *which he extended to include religious behaviour and a recommendation to read good recent literature: works by Gower, Chaucer, Hoccleve, and Lydgate. Here he describes how a boy of rank – such as a gentleman's or merchant's son – should pray when he gets up every morning:*

Afore all things, first and principally,
In the morning when you shall uprise,
God's worship must be in your memory.
First, cross yourself for blessing; do it thrice,
Then *Paternoster*[1] say in devout wise,[2]
Ave Maria, and the holy Creed,
That all day long the better may you speed.

And while you are engaging busily
To dress yourself and put on your array,
With your companion, obediently,
I strongly recommend that you should say
Our Lady's matins every single day,
With prime and hours.[3] Do not fear the task;
Our Lady then will grant you what you ask.

He also gives advice on what to do in church.

When you arrive at church, my little child,
Holy water you should upon you cast.
Approach the cross[4] in mood most meek and mild,
Then kneel and knock your fist upon your breast,
Thanking the Lord who on the cross did rest

---

1 The Lord's Prayer, followed by the Hail Mary and the Apostles' Creed, all said in Latin. 2 Manner. 3 Our Lady's matins, prime, and hours were contained in the Book of Hours; they were simple services in Latin or English for lay people. 4 The great crucifix above the rood screen, at the east end of the nave of the church.

And there for you suffered his heart to bleed,
Saying a *Pater*, *Ave*, and a Creed.

Remember too, on top of everything,
A church should be a house of prayer, a place
Where there should be no clap or jangling;[1]
To make a noise in church is very base,
And shows that they who do so have no grace,
So be demure and silent; it makes sense
To serve your God with all your diligence.

If it should happen when the priest says mass,
That you are picked to serve him at his side,
Do not creep off or from his presence pass,
But kneel or stand devoutly – as a guide
Close by but not too near. Be not tongue-tied,
But when you make responses, make them clear,
So any who are listening can hear.

DINNER AT A BOARDING SCHOOL

During the fifteenth century, another adaptation was made of Stans
Puer ad Mensam *into rhymed Latin verse. The poem, known as* Castrianus, *consists of 150 lines composed in a single day (quite an
achievement), and was probably written for either Winchester College
or Eton College: the only two large boarding schools then in existence.
In this excerpt from the poem, the writer lays down how dinner should
be eaten in the college hall, with the college clergy and schoolmasters
in charge and over a hundred boys sitting at the tables:*

All who come to dinner must wash their hands routinely,
And ensure that all their knives are both sharp and cleanly.
While we[2] sit in presence here, do not leave your places
Till you stand and all recite the concluding graces;

---

1 Noise and disturbance.   2 The headmaster.

If you should be by yourselves, say them in rotation,
One of you each day, to show your appreciation.
When you sit around the board, all of you are equal,
Friendship then with everyone is the rightful sequel.

When you talk at dinner time, in your places sitting,
Latin must alone be used; English is not fitting.
Conversation should be low, peace predominating,
Stories that are lecherous nobody narrating.
Readings from the Bible or from some other matter
Should not be disrupted by rant or idle chatter.

When it happens that at meals soup has been provided,
Do not drink as gluttons do, or you will be chided.
Make sure that your spoon is clean, use it elegantly;
Never in the empty dish leave it nonchalantly.
Courtesy demands respect in another matter:
That your head is never bent downwards to the platter.
Take a trencher and with care cut the food before you
So as not to mark your clothes, else we shall deplore you;

The remainder of your meal lay out providently
On a portion of your bread placed conveniently.
Previous to taking drink, wipe your hands precisely,
And to make the trencher clean, crumbs will help you nicely.
Never put large mouthfuls in for your mastication,
So that you may answer if there is conversation.
Never seek to pick your teeth while at table feeding;
To expose your gums will shock people of good breeding.
When at table, knife to mouth never must be taken,
And by hands at other times both should be forsaken.

Feasts are best when we are kept in anticipation;
Touching dishes early is yielding to temptation.
Even though you find a dish specially enticing,
It is meant for all around, everyone sufficing;
They are rude and rustic who munch away uncaring
At the dishes that they take which are meant for sharing;
Take care, then, in following such a bad example;
Let the rest have pleasure in those things that you sample.

When you cut a dish of meat, sawing is not fitting;
He should be ashamed who saws while that he is sitting.
Clean your knife in readiness to dissect the cheeses;
Separately, not at once, gather up the pieces.
Mouth and table never should come into conjunction,
Nor let singing, like a fool, ever be your function.
If your trencher comes to be sullied with pollution,
Place another one on top; that is the solution.
Fatty cheese you should not taste, and we do deplore it;
It is not a seemly dish, so we say ignore it.

When the time allowed to eat reaches termination,
Knives must then be scraped to clean any encrustation. . . . .
Water being carried in, all must rise in motion,
Rendering their thanks to God with a keen devotion.
If a boy is table-head, minister the water,
Genuflecting carefully, as if at the altar;
Offer him the bowl or cloth to allow ablution,
And bring every other task to a resolution.
But while you remain in hall, we again remind you
To pronounce the grace in turn; to that end we bind you.
None of you should be in doubt: praising our Creator
Will the better expedite our endeavours later.

BEHAVIOUR FOR GIRLS

The Good Wife Taught her Daughter *is one of the few surviving courtesy poems for girls. It was written in the mid fourteenth century, probably in the Midlands and supposedly by a woman for her daughter. Since the girl is envisaged as having a household of servants but helping at times with the housework, the poem was aimed at the daughters of citizens or wealthy yeomen farmers rather than those of the nobility and gentry. Each stanza is followed by a proverb. The author expected a woman to lead a restricted and submissive way of life by modern standards!*

Daughter, if thou wilt be a wife and wise in thy work,
See that thou love full well God and Holy Church.
Go to church when thou mayst, stay not home for the rain;
All day thou farest better when thou hast God seen.[1]
 Well thriveth that God loveth.

Blithely give thy tithes and thy offerings[2] both;
To help the poor at thy gate, do not be loth;
Give them charity blithely, do not be too hard;
Seldom is the house poor where God is steward.
 Well hath that poor relieveth.

While thou sittest in church, thy beads thou shalt bid,[3]
Make no jangling[4] with stranger or with sib,[5]
Laugh not at anyone, either old or young,
But be of good bearing and of good tongue.
 In thy good bearing begins thine honour.

If any man gives thee honour and offers to wed thee,
Answer him sweetly; scorn him not, whoever he be.
Discuss it with thy family and conceal it not,
Meanwhile sit not nor stand by him, lest sin be wrought.
 A slander raised is hard to still.

When a man weds thee before God with a ring,
Look that thou bow to him and love him over everything.
Answer him meekly without snapping or snarling,
And so thou shalt soften his mood and be his darling.
 Fair words slacken wrath.

Sweet of speech shalt thou be, glad and mild of mood,
True in word and deed, in life and soul good.

---

1 i.e. the image of Christ on the crucifix in church. 2 Offerings of money in church four times a year. 3 Use the rosary, saying a prayer as you hold each bead. 4 Conversation. 5 Your family members.

Keep thyself from sin, villainy, and blame,
And bear thee so that folk say of thee no shame.
   Good life winneth well.

Be of fair appearance and of good manner,
Change not thy countenance for anything thou may hear;
Behave not as a gig[1] for anything that may betide,[2]
Nor laugh not too loud, nor yawn thou too wide.
   Laugh and make a fair mouth.

When thou goest on the road, go thou not too fast;
Toss not thy head or thy shoulders up-cast,[3]
Be not of many words, nor too greatly swear,
All such manners, daughter, avoid everywhere.
   Bad manners, bad name.

Go not to town like a gadabout, or run
From one house to another looking for fun;
Go not even to market, thy cloth to sell,
Or to a tavern – that will shame thee as well.
   Tavern going is thrift's undoing.

And if thou be in any house where good drink is aloft,
Whether thou serve it or sit quietly and soft,
Take of it in measure, that there comes to thee no blame,
For if thou art often drunk, it will be to thy shame.
   Measure and skill oft have their will.

Go not to wrestlings or shooting at a cock,
In the way of a strumpet or a gigelot.[4]
Stay at home, daughter, within thy own pitch,
And so thou shalt, my dear child, soon grow rich.[5]
   Keep thine own and be merry.

---

1 Giddy woman.   2 Happen.   3 Shrug.   4 A loose gadabout girl.   5 Another
manifestation of the 'Protestant ethic'.

Greet not every man thou meetest in the street;
Though he addresses thee, shortly him greet.
Let him go by the way, by him do not stay,
Lest he change thy heart by any villainy.
   All is not true that is fair spoken.

Do not for covetousness any gift take;
Unless thou know why it is given, soon it forsake;
Good wise men have, with gifts, been undone,
Although they were as true as wood or stone.
   Gift taking is bond-making.

In other folks' houses do not seek for mastery;
Blame nothing there that thou seest with thine eye.
Daughter, I pray thee, behave thee so well
That all may say thou art as true as steel.
   A good name is worth gold.

Be thou no scolder, nor of words bold
To abuse thy neighbours, neither young nor old;
Be not too moody, nor too envious,
Whatever may happen in another's house.
   An envious heart frets itself apart.

And if thy neighbour's wife have rich attire,
Make no strife about it or burn as if with fire,
But thank God for whatever goods that he to thee shall give,
And so, my dear child, a good life thou shalt live.
   He is at ease that seldom thanketh.

Be like a housewife on a working day;
Pride, rest, and idleness – put them all away,
Then when a holiday comes, well shalt thou be
To honour the holiday, and God shall love thee.
   More comes from honour than from pride.

With rich robes and garlands and any such thing,
Do not counterfeit a lady, as if thy lord were a king;
With what he may provide, satisfied shalt thou be,
Lest he lose his reputation for love of thee.
    Overmuch pride brings a naked side.

Much shame may they have, and so them betide,
That make their lords poor with overmuch pride,
Be wise, daughter, and a housewife good:
In a wren's veins there is only so much blood.[1]
    Spend more than you win, and thrift grows thin.

Wisely look after thy house and thy meinie,[2]
And neither too bitter nor too sweet with them be.
See whatever work most needs to be done,
And set them to do it both quickly and soon.
    Ready is at need before a done deed.

And if thy lord be away, let them not go idle;
Make sure that thou knowest who does much or little;
Reward whoever works well and is willing;
He will do better another time, unless he is a villain.
    Before a done deed another makes speed.

And if thy need be great and help is short,
Go thyself and do a housewife's work:
They will do better if their mistress by them stands;
Work is done sooner by many hands.
    Many hands make light work.

See what thy household does, and about them go;
When each thing is done, be thou there also.
If thou find them at fault, soon make them amend,

---

1 A proverb: cut your coat according to the cloth.   2 Household including servants.

Unless there is an excuse that may them defend.
Much work he knows who keeps a house.

Look that all be well when work must be stopped;
Keep the keys in thy care, not forgotten or dropped;
Look that all be well; spare not thy energies,
And if thou dost so, daughter, thou dost like the wise.
Love none better than thyself.

Borrow not too blithely nor run up a debt,
Unless a great need or great want must be met;
Make not thyself rich from someone else's things,
Rather than spend a couple of farthings.
Borrowed things will come home.

If thou love thy children well, keep them under control;
If any misbehave, do not curse them or bawl,
But take a smart rod and beat them in a row
Till they cry mercy and their misdeeds show.
Loved child needs learning.

Now have I taught thee, daughter, as did my mother me,
Think thereon night and day: forget not these three –
Measure, humility, forethought – that I have thee taught,
And the man that thou weddest shall regret naught.
Better unborn than of teaching forlorn.

Now may thrift and prosperity be thine, my dear,
And from all our forefathers that were or are,
And from patriarchs and prophets that ever were alive,
Blessings may thou have, and may thou well thrive!
The child that thrives, well is he.

HUNTING

*Several handbooks on hunting were written in the Middle Ages.
This one*, Tristram, *takes its name from a hero of twelfth-century*

romances, who was believed to have been an expert on hunting procedures. It was composed in verse in the fifteenth century, or perhaps the late fourteenth, allegedly by a gentlewoman for her son: a teenager strong enough to ride and hunt. She may have been called Julian Barnes, but has never been identified. The poem was printed in a treatise called The Book of St Albans *in 1486 and was widely read thereafter. What follow are the opening and some extracts:*

Wheresoever you fare, by frith or by fell,[1]
My dear child, take heed how Tristram doth you tell
How many beasts of venery there were,
Listen to your dame and then you shall hear.
Four manners of beasts of venery there are:
The first of them is the hart, the second is the hare,
The others are the boar,
The wolf and no more.

And where that you come in plain or in place,
I shall tell you which be the beasts of the chase:
One of them is the buck, another is the doe,
The fox and the marten, and the wild roe,
And my dear child, you shall other beasts all
Wheresoever you find them, 'rascal' them call,
In frith or in fell,
Or in forest as I tell. . . .

The mother explains the terms for deer of different ages:

And for to speak of the hart, if you will it hear,
You shall call him a calf at the first year,
The second year a brocket, so shall you him call,
The third year a spayad: learn these words all;
The fourth year a stag, call him by any way,

---

1 Frith and fell: wood and hillside.

The fifth year a great stag, your dame bids you say,
The sixth year, call you him a hart;
Do so, my child, while you be alert.

And the proper way to refer to groups of animals:

My child, talk of 'herds' of hart and of hind
And of buck and of doe where you shall them find,
And a 'bevy' of roes, what place they be in,
And call it a 'sounder' of the wild swine,
And a 'rout' of wolves wherever you come in;
These beasts all,
Thus shall you them call. . . .

She describes the best times of the year for hunting different animals:

The 'time of grease'[1] begins at Midsummer Day
And lasts till Holy Rood Day, as I you say;
The season of the fox from the Nativity
To the Annunciation of Our Lady free;
The season of the roebuck at Easter shall begin
And till Michaelmas lasteth before it falls in;
The season of the roe beginneth at Michaelmas,
And it shall endure and last till Candlemas;
At Michaelmas beginneth hunting of the hare
And lasts till Midsummer, no man it will spare;
The season of the wolf is in each country
As the season of the fox, and evermore shall be;
The season of the boar is from the Nativity
Till the Purification of Our Lady so free. . . .

She explains how to organise a hunt: this part relates to hunting the hare. It shows that French was still used for speaking to the hounds,

---

1 This relates to the hunting of deer.

in fact a kind of dog-French, reminding us that for a long time after 1066, hunting in England was dominated by the French-speaking aristocracy:

Now to speak of the hare, how all shall be wrought,
When she with hounds be found and fought.
The first word to the hounds that the hunter shall output
Is at the kennel door when he opens it.
So that all may hear,
He shall say *Arere*,[1]
For his hounds would come out too hastily;
That is the first word, my son, of venery,
And when he has coupled his hounds each one
And is forth with them to the field gone,
And when he has cast off his couples at will
Then shall he speak and say his hounds till,[2]
Hors de couple! Auaunt, sirs, auaunt[3] twice so,
And then *So ho, so ho*, thrice and no more,
And then *Sa sa cy auaunt*,[4] high and not low,
And then *Sa cy avant, sa cy avant, so ho!*
And if you see your hounds have good will to run
And draw away from you, say as I you ken,[5]
Here how amy,[6] again call them so,
Then *Sweff mon amy, sweff*,[7] to make them soft go,
And if any find of the hare where he has been
And be called Richer or Beaumont, thus let it be bidden:
'*Oyes a Beamont le vaillant* and I shall you avow
Que quida trou la cowarde ou la court cowe,'
Meaning, 'Beaumont, be it you without any fail,
Who finds the coward[8] with the short tail!'

There are rather gory instructions about how the chief hunter should carve up an animal after it is killed. He should take part for

---

1 Back! 2 Say to his hounds. 3 Uncouple [them]! On, sirs, on! 4 Here, here, come on! 5 Teach you. 6 Here, friend! 7 Gently, my friend! 8 i.e. the hare.

himself and give rewards to the foresters who helped organise the hunt. In this passage the animal is a hart (a six year-old deer). The hunt ends with the hunters ceremoniously taking back the deer carcass to the house of the lord of the forest:

> Who dresses the hart,[1] by my counsel,
> Shall have the left shoulder for his travail,
> And the right shoulder, wheresoever he be,
> Give to the forester, for that is his fee,
> And the liver also of the same beast
> To the forester's man, give at the least.
> Truss the numbles[2] in the skin and secure it fast;
> Let the sides and the haunches together be cast
> With the hind legs; be done so it shall,
> Then bring it home and the skin with all
> The numbles and the horns to the lord's gate,
> Then boldly blow the 'prise'[3] thereat,
> To proclaim your win
> Before you come in.

---

1 The chief hunter who cuts it up.   2 Intestines.   3 The announcement of a successful hunt.

STORIES

Children must often have been present when adults told stories by mouth or read them aloud from books. By the fifteenth century, there is evidence that many were gaining access to written stories more directly. Educational writers began to advise them to read Gower, Chaucer, and some of the romances, and books began to be produced or adapted especially for them. Three of these stories, all poems, are featured in the following pages.

Some of the most popular works of the fifteenth and sixteenth centuries were ballads about Robin Hood. We know that this also applied to young people, because writers of a strict disposition denounced the fact. The Bible translator William Tyndale, for example, included Robin Hood among tales that he called 'as filthy as heart can think to corrupt the minds of youth'. From about 1500, it was possible to buy the longest ballad, *A Lytell Gest of Robyn Hode*, in a printed version for a few pence, and this must have become well known to children and teenagers. It is too long to print as a whole, so Part 5 of it has been chosen for its portrayal of a typically thrilling encounter between Robin and the Sheriff of Nottingham.

Sir *Aldingar* is a type of folk-story found in the literature of many countries. A virtuous woman is falsely accused of a crime, condemned to death, and finally rescued. In England, the poem is first recorded in the famous Percy Folio of about 1650, but it shows signs of being much older. The request of the dying villain to receive immediate communion from a priest suggests an origin before the Reformation, and there are places where words have been changed, presumably because they were old and no longer understandable. In any case, it is a traditional kind of tale that would have been told in families with children listening, or even told to children on their own because it features a boy as the hero.

The Friar and the Boy, also known as *Jack and his Stepdame*, is a fifteenth-century story, and surely chiefly for children rather than adults. It is a rollicking tale in verse about a boy Jack, which makes no attempt to teach anything other than to be generous rather than spiteful. It was first printed by Wynkyn de Worde in London between 1510 and 1513, with a pretty woodcut showing Jack piping while he keeps his cows. The work was a great success and was reprinted several times down to the early nineteenth century. It is a little too long (and perhaps too bald at times) to be included here completely, so that some of the action has been abridged in prose.

ROBIN HOOD

From Part Five of A Lytell Gest of Robyn Hode. *The story so far: Robin has lent money to Sir Richard at the Lee, a knight who is down on his luck. The outlaws have also captured the Sheriff of Nottingham but have released him in return for his solemn oath that he will never again do them harm:*

>Lithe[1] and listen, gentlemen,
>   And hearken what I shall say,
>How the proud sheriff of Nottingham
>   Proclaimed a full fair play,

---

1 Hearken.

That all the best archers of the north
   Should come upon a day,
And they that shot the best of all
   The game should bear away.

He that shoots the best of all,
   Farthest, fair, and low,
At a pair of goodly butts[1]
   Under the greenwood shaw,[2]

A right good arrow he shall have,
   The shaft of silver white,
The head and the feathers of rich red gold,
   In England is none like.

This then heard good Robin,
   Under his trysting tree,[3]
'Make you ready, you bold young men,
   That shooting will I see.

'Make ready, my merry young men,
   Ye shall go with me,
And I will know the sheriff's faith,
   If he be true to me.'

When they had their bows bent,
   Their arrows feathered free,
Seven score of bold young men
   Stood by Robin's knee.

When they came to Nottingham,
   The butts were fair and long;
Many was the bold archer
   That shot with bows strong.

---

1 Targets.   2 Another word for 'wood'.   3 The tree where he and the outlaws met.

'There shall but six shoot with me;
   The others shall guard my head,
And stand with good bows bent
   That I be not deceived.'

The fourth outlaw his bow did bend,
   And that was Robin Hood,
And he was spied by the proud sheriff
   As by the butts he stood.

Thrice Robin shot about,
   And always he hit the wand,
And so did good Gilbert
   With the white hand.

Little John and good Scarlet
   Were archers good and free;
Little Much and good Reynold
   The worst would they not be.

When they had shot about,
   These archers fair and good,
Evermore the best one was
   For truth, Robin Hood.

He was given the good arrow,
   For best worthy was he;
He took the gift so courteously,
   Then to greenwood would he.

But they cried out ''Tis Robin Hood!',
   And great horns did they blow.
'Woe to thee, treason!' said Robin,
   'Full evil thou art to know.

'And woe to thee, proud sheriff,
   To gladden thus thy guest;
In other wise thou promised me
   In yonder wild forest.

'But had I thee in the greenwood,
    Under my trysting tree,
Thou shouldst leave me a better pledge
    Than thy true loyalty.'

Full many a bow there was bent,
    And arrows let they glide;
Many a short coat there was rent,
    And hurt was many a side.

The outlaws shot was so strong
    That none might them outlast,
And the proud sheriff's men
    They fled away full fast.

Robin saw the ambush had failed,
    In greenwood he would be;
Many an arrow there was shot
    Among that company,

But Little John was hurt full sore
    With an arrow in his knee,
That he might neither walk not ride;
    It was a great pity.

'Master', then said Little John,
    'If ever thou lovest me,
And for Our Lord's love
    That died upon a tree,

'And for the reward of my service
    That I have given thee,
Never let the proud sheriff
    Alive now find me.

'But take out thy bright sword,
    And smite off all my head,

And give me wounds deep and wide,
    Until that I am dead.

'I would not that', said Robin,
    'John, that thou were slain,
For all the gold in merry England
    And all of it again.'

'God forbid', said little Much,
    'He that died on a tree,
That thou shouldst ever, Little John,
    Part from our company.'

Up he took him on his back
    And bore him well a mile;
Many a time he laid him down
    And shot another while.

Nearby there was a fair castle,
    A little within the wood,
Double ditched it was around,
    And walled, by the Rood.[1]

And there dwelt that gentle knight.
    Sir Richard at the Lee,
To whom Robin had lent money
    Under the greenwood tree.

In he took good Robin
    And all his company,
'Welcome be thou, Robin Hood,
    Welcome art thou to me.

'And much I thank thee for thy comfort
    And for thy courtesy,
And for thy great kindness
    Under the greenwood tree.

---

1 By God's Holy Cross – a statement of emphasis.

'I love no man in all this world
    So much as I do thee,
And for all the proud sheriff of Nottingham,
    Right safe here shalt thou be.

'Shut the gates and draw the bridge,
    And let no man come in,
And arm yourselves, make ready
    And to guard the walls begin!'

SIR ALDINGAR

Some lines of the poem are missing, and I have filled the gaps
with new ones in italics.

Sir Aldingar's plot:

Our king he kept a false steward,
    Men called him Sir Aldingar;
A keen knight, with a comely face,
    And a heart as black as tar.

He would have lain by our comely queen,
    Her honour to betray;
Our queen, she was a good woman
    And evermore said him nay.

Aldingar was offended in his mind,
    With her he was never content,
But he sought what means he could find out
    In a fire to have her brent.[1]

There came a lame lazar[2] to the king's gates,
    A lazar blind and lame;

---

1 Burnt. 2 Leper.

He took the lazar upon his back
   On the queen's bed he was lain.

He said, 'Lie still, lazar, as thou liest;
   Look thou go not away;
I'll make thee a whole man and a sound
   In two hours of a day.'

And then went forth Sir Aldingar,
   Our queen for to betray,
And then he met with our comely king,
   Says, 'God you save and see!

'If I had space, as I have grace,
   A message I would say to thee.'
'Say on, say on, Sir Aldingar,
   Say on and unto me.'

'I can show you one of the grievousest sights
   That a Christian king did see;
Our queen hath chosen a new, new love,
   She will have none of thee.

'If she had chosen a right good knight,
   The less had been her shame,
But she hath chosen a lazar man
   Who is both blind and lame.'

'If this be true, thou Aldingar,
   That thou dost tell to me,
Then I will make thee a rich knight,
   Both of gold and fee.

'But if it be false, Sir Aldingar,
   That thou dost tell to me,
Then look for no other death
   But to be hanged on a tree.

Go with me', said our comely king,
   'This lazar for to see.'

The wrath of King Henry:

When the king he came into the queen's chamber,
   Standing her bed before,
'There is a loathly rogue', says Harry King,
   'For our dame Queen Elinor!'

'If thou were a man, as thou art none,
   Here thou shouldest be slain;
But a pair of new gallows shall be built,
   Thou 'lt hang on them so high.

'And a fair fire there shall be made,
   And brent our queen shall be.'
Forthwith then walked our comely king
   And met with our comely queen.

Says, 'God you save, our queen, madam,
   And Christ you save and see!
Here you have chosen a new, new love,
   And you will have none of me.

'If you had chosen a right good knight,
   The less had been your shame,
But you have chosen a lazar man,
   That is both blind and lame.'

'Ever alack!' said our comely queen,
   'Sir Aldingar is false to me,
But ever alack!' said our comely queen,
   'Ever alas, and woe is me!'

'I had thought dreams had never been true;
   I have proved them true at the last;

I dreamt in my dream on Thursday at even[1]
　　In my bed whereas I lay,

'I dreamt a griffin, a grimly beast,
　　Had carried my crown away,
My gorget[2] and my kirtle[3] of gold,
　　And all my fair headgear.

'How he would have worried me with his tooth,
　　And borne me into his nest,
Saving there came a little hawk,
　　Flying out of the east.

'Saving there came a little hawk
　　Which men call a merlion;[4]
Until the ground he struck him down,
　　That dead he did fall down.

'If I were a man, as I am none,
　　A battle I would prove;
I would fight with that false traitor;
　　At him I cast my glove!

'Seeing I am able no battle to make,
　　You must grant me, my liege, a knight
To fight with that traitor, Sir Aldingar,
　　To maintain me in my right.'

'I'll give thee forty days', said our king,
　　'To seek thee a man therein;
If thou find not a man in forty days,
　　In a hot fire thou shall burn.'

---

1 Evening.　2 Collar or necklace.　3 Gown or robe.　4 A merlin, a small hawk.

The search for a champion:

Our queen sent forth a messenger;
    He rode fast into the south;
He rode the countries through and through,
    So far unto Portsmouth.

But though he rode from town to town,
    And house to house, I ween,[1]
He could never find a man in the south country
    That would fight the knight so keen.

The second messenger the queen forth sent
    Rode far into the east;
But blessed be God, made sun and moon,
    He sped then all of the best.

As he rode then by one river side,
    There he met with a little child;
He seemed no more in a man's likeness
    Than a child of four years old.

He asked the queen's messenger how far he rode;
    Loth he was him to tell;
The little one was offended at him,
    Bid him 'Adieu, farewell.'

Said, 'Turn thou again, thou messenger,
    Greet our queen well from me;
When bale is highest, boot is next;[2]
    Help enough there may be.

'Bid our queen remember what she did dream
    In her bed whereas she lay;

---

1 I believe.   2 A proverb: when trouble is worst, reward is near.

She dreamed the griffin, the grimly beast,
    Had carried her crown away;

'Her gorget and her kirtle of gold,
    Also her fair headgear;
He would have worried her with his tooth,
    And borne her into his nest.

'Saving there came a little hawk,
    Men call him a merlion;
Unto the ground he did strike him down,
    That dead he did fall down.

'Bid the queen be merry at her heart,
    Evermore light and glad;
When bale is highest, boot is next;
    Help enough there shall be.'

Then the queen's messenger rode back,
    A gladded man then was he;
When he came before our queen,
    A glad woman then was she.

She gave the messenger twenty pound,
    O lord, in gold and fee;
Says, 'Spend and spare not while this doth last,
    Then fetch thou more of me.'

The rescue of the queen:

Our queen was put in a tun[1] to burn;
    She thought no thing but death;
Then they were ware of the little one
    Came riding forth of the east,

---

1 Barrel.

With a morion helm and armour bright,
    A lovely child was he;
When he came to that fire,
    He alighted the queen full nigh.

Said, 'Draw away these brands of fire
    Lie burning before our queen,
And fetch me hither Sir Aldingar,
    That is a knight so keen.'

When Aldingar saw that little one,
    Full little of him he thought;
If there had been half a hundred such,
    Of them he would not have wrought.

He said, 'Come hither, Sir Aldingar;
    Thou seemest as big as a fother;[1]
I trust to God, ere I have done with thee
    God will send to us an augure.'[2]

Says, 'The first stroke that's given, Sir Aldingar,
    I will give unto thee,
And if the second give thou may,
    Look then thou spare not me.'

The little one pulled forth a well good sword,
    Iwis[3] it was all of gilt;
It cast light there over that field,
    Shining from point to hilt.

He struck the first stroke at Aldingar;
    He struck his legs by his knee;
And Aldingar fell on the ground,
    Full sorely hurt was he.

---

1 Cartload or large weight.   2 Omen.   3 Indeed.

Says, 'Stand up, stand up, thou false traitor,
    And fight upon thy feet;
For and thou thrive as thou begins,
    Of a height we shall be meet.'[1]

'A priest! A priest!' says Aldingar,
    'Me for to housel and shrive![2]
A priest! A priest!' says Aldingar,
    'While I am a man alive![3]

'I would have lain by our comely queen;
    To it she would never consent;
I thought to have betrayed her to our king,
    In a fire to have had her brent.

'There came a lame lazar to the king's gate,
    A lazar both blind and lame;
I took the lazar upon my back,
    In the queen's bed he was lain.

'I bade him, Lie still lazar, where he lay,
    Look he went not away;
I would make him a whole man and a sound
    In two hours of a day.

And then I brought our comely king,
    And lies to him did tell.
Ever alack!' says Sir Aldingar,
    'Falseness never does well.

'Forgive, forgive me, queen, madam,
    For Christ's love forgive me!'
'God forgave his death, Aldingar,
    And freely I forgive thee.'

---

1 Equal.   2 Give me holy communion and hear my confession.   3 Give holy communion.

'Now take thy wife, thou King Harry,
    And love her now thou shall;
Thy wife she is as true to thee
    As stone on castle wall.'

The lazar under the gallow tree
    Was a pretty man and small;
The lazar under the gallow tree
    Was made steward in King Henry's hall.

THE FRIAR AND THE BOY

Here beginneth a merry jest of the friar and the boy

God that died for us all,
And drank both eisell[1] and gall,
Bring us out of bale,[2]
And give them good life and long
That listeneth to my song,
Or attendeth to my tale.

There dwelt a farmer in my country,
That had wives three
In the course of time;
By the first wife a son he had,
That was a good sturdy lad,
And a happy hind.[3]

His father loved him well;
His stepmother never a deal;
I tell you as I think.
All she thought was lost, by the Rood,
That did the little boy any good,
Whether in meat or drink,

---

1 Vinegar.   2 Trouble.   3 Boy.

And yet iwis[1] it was but bad,
And thereof not half enough he had,
But evermore of the worst.
Therefore evil may she fare,
For ever she did the little boy care,[2]
As far forth as she durst.

The goodwife to her man did say,
'I would you would put this boy away,
And that right soon in haste.
Truly he is a cursed lad;
I would some other man him had,
That would him better chaste.[3]'

Then said the good man again,
'Dame, I shall to thee say plain,
He is but tender of age.
He shall abide with me this year
Till he be more stronger
For to earn better wage.

'We have a man, a stout freke,[4]
That in the field keepeth our neat,[5]
Sleeping all the day.
He shall come home, so God me shield,
And the boy shall into the field
To keep our beasts if he may.

Then said the wife, 'Verily,
Thereto soon I do agree,
For that me thinketh most needy.'
On the morrow when it was day,
Jack the boy went on his way
To the field full ready.

---

1 Indeed.   2 Sorrow.   3 Chastise.   4 Another word for man.   5 Cattle.

Of no man he had a care,
But sang 'Hey, ho, away the mare',[1]
And made joy enough.
Forth he went, truly to say,
Till he came to the plain;
His dinner forth he drew.

When he saw it was but bad,
Full little lust thereto he had,
But put it up again,
Therefore he was not too keen,
He said that he would stay but lean
Till night when he came home.

And as the boy sat on a hill,
An old man came him till,
Walking by the way.
Soon he said, 'God thee see'.
'Sir, welcome may you be',
The little boy did say.

The old man said, 'I am hungry sore,
Hast thou any meat in store
That thou mayst give me?'
The child said, 'So God me save,
Such little victual as I have,
Welcome shall ye be.'

The old man eats Jack's lunch and asks him to choose three gifts in return:

'Son, thou hast given meat to me;
I shall give thee things three;
Thou shalt them never forget.'

---

1 Perhaps a lost song, with a catch-phrase meaning, 'have no care'.

Then said the boy, 'As I trow,[1]
It is best that I have a bow
Birds for to shoot.'

'A bow, son, I shall thee give
That shall last thee all thy life
And never a like one meet.
Shoot therein when thou good think,
For if thou shoot and wink,
The prick thou shalt hit.'

When Jack the bow in hand felt,
And the bolts[2] under his belt,
Loud then he did laugh.
He said, 'Now had I a pipe,
Though it were never so light,
Then were I glad enough.'

'A pipe, son, thou shalt have also
In true music it shall go,
I do thee well to wit.
All that may the pipe hear,
Shall not themselves steer,
But laugh and leap about.

'What shall the third be,
For I will give thee gifts three
As I have said to thee before?'
The little boy to him did laugh,
And said 'Sir I have enough;
I will desire no more.'

The old man said, 'My truth I plight.
Thou shalt have that I thee hight,[3]

---

1 Think.   2 Arrows.   3 Told you.

Say on now, and let me see.'
Then said the boy anon,
'I have a stepdame at home;
She is a shrew to me.

'When my father giveth me meat,
She would thereon that I would choke,
And stareth me in the face.
When she looketh on me so,
I would she should let a rap go[1]
That it might ring over all the place.'

Jack takes the gifts and goes home:

He took his pipe and began to blow;
All his beasts on a row,
About him they dance.
Thus went he piping through the town
His beasts him followed by the sound
Into his father's close.

His father at his supper sat,
Little Jack espied well that,
And said to him anon,
'Father I have kept your neat;
I pray you give me some meat.
I am hungered, by St John. . . .'

His father took a capon's wing,
And at the boy he did it fling,
And bade him eat apace.
That grieved his stepmother's heart sore,
As I told you before;
She stared him in the face.

---

1 Break wind.

With that she let go a blast,
That they in the hall were aghast:
It rang all over the place.
All they laughed and had good game;
The wife waxed red for shame;
She wished she were somewhere else.

Afterwards as you shall hear
To the house there came a friar
To lie there all night.
The wife loved him as a saint,
And to him made her complaint,
And told him aright,

'We have a boy within iwis,
A villain for the nonce[1] he is
He brings me much care.
I dare not look him upon;
I am ashamed, by St John,
To tell you how I fare.

'I pray you meet the boy tomorrow;
Beat him well and give him sorrow,
And make the boy lame.'
Quoth the friar, 'I shall him beat.'
Quoth the wife, 'Do not forget;
He doth me much shame.'

Next day the friar goes out to the fields where Jack is keeping the animals:

When he came upon the land,
Little Jack there he found
Driving his beasts alone.

---

1 Every time.

'Boy', he said, 'God give thee shame.
What hast thou done to thy dame?
Tell thou me anon.

'Unless thou canst excuse thee well,
By my troth I beat thee will;
I will no longer abide.'[1]
Quoth the boy, 'What aileth thee?
My dame fareth as well as ye,
What needeth thee to chide?'

Quoth the boy, 'Will ye know
How I can shoot birds with my bow,
And other things withal?
Although I be but small of height,
Yonder bird will I smite,
And give her thee I shall.'

There sat a bird upon a briar.
'Shoot on, boy', quoth the friar,
'For that I long to see.'
Jack hit the bird upon the head,
And at once she fell down dead,
No further might she flee.

The friar to the bush he went,
To take the bird was his intent,
Now that he had the chance.
Jack took his pipe and began to blow,
Then the friar as I trow,
Began at once to dance.

As soon as he the pipe heard,
Like a madman he fared;

---

1 I won't wait any longer.

He leapt and danced about.
The briars scratched him in the face
And in many another place,
So that the blood burst out,

They tore his clothes relentlessly,
His cape and his scapulary,[1]
And all his robes indeed.
He danced among the thorns so thick,
In many places they did him prick;
He fast began to bleed.

Jack piped and laughed, as in among
The thorns the friar was scratched and stung;
He hopped wondrously high,
At last the friar held up his hand
And said 'I have danced so long
That I am like to die.

'Gentle Jack, hold thy pipe still,
I promise I'll do thee no ill,
Indeed I'll swear it so.'
So Jack put down the pipe and cried,
'Friar, skip out the further side,
And lightly leap to go.'

The friar out of the bush went,
All to-ragged and to-rent,
And torn on every side.
Was scarcely left on him one clout
His belly for to wrap about,
His harness for to hide.

*The friar goes back to the house in a rage and complains about
Jack. When Jack gets home his father wants to know more about*

---

1 Cloak.

*the marvellous pipe. As soon as Jack begins to play, everyone
starts dancing:*

> As soon as Jack began to blow,
> All that were there were, I tell you true,
> Began to dance and leap.
> When they began the pipe to hear,
> They might not themselves steer,
> But tumbled in a heap.
>
> The farmer was in no despair,
> But lightly leapt out of his chair,
> With a good cheer;
> Some leapt over the stock,
> Some stumbled at the block,
> And some fell flat in the fire.
>
> The farmer thought it was a game
> How they danced all the same;
> His wife too had to step.
> Evermore she kept her eye on Jack,
> And fast her tail began to crack,
> Louder than they could speak. . . .
>
> Jack ran into the street,
> After him fast did they leap,
> Truly they could not stint.
> They went out at the door so thick
> That each fell on the others' neck,
> So prettily out they went.
>
> The neighbours that were living by,
> Heard the pipe go so merrily,
> They ran out of the gate.
> Some leapt over the hatch,
> They had no time to draw the latch;
> They thought they were too late.

Some were sleeping in their bed,
But they held up their head;
Anon they were awakèd;
Then they danced from where they lay
Truly as I you say,
Stark belly naked.

By that time there was all about
The neighbourhood iwis[1] a rout
All dancing in the street.
Some were lame and might not go,
But iwis they were dancing too,
On their hands and feet.

*The friar is so angry that he summons Jack before the Official,
the judge of the Church court, on a charge of doing magic. The
stepmother turns up as a witness:*

Friday came, as you may hear;
Jack's stepdame and the friar,
Together there they met.
Folk gathered with a lively pace,
And, to hear of every case,
The Official was set.

There was much to do,
Matters more than one or two,
Both with priest and clerk;
Some had testaments[2] to prove;
And fair women, by your leave,
That had strokes in the dark.[3]

Everyone put forth his case;
Then came forth Friar Topias

---

1 Indeed.   2 Wills.   3 Church courts dealt with sexual crimes.

And Jack's stepdame also.
'Sir Official', said he,
'I have brought a boy to thee
Who hath wrought me woe.

'He is a great necromancer
In all Orleans is not his peer,
As by my truth I trow.'
'He is a witch', quoth the wife,
Then – what happened next is blithe –
Loud she began to blow.

Some laughed and did not fail,
Some said 'Dame, temper thy tail,
You wrest it all amiss.'
'Dame', quoth the Official
Go on giving us thy tale,
And do not stop for this.'

The Official demands to hear the pipe as well:

'Pipe on, Jack', said the Official,
'I will hear now how thou canst play.'
Jack blew his pipe, the truth to say,
And made them to dance all.

The Official leapt over the desk,[1]
And danced about wondrous fast,
Till both his shins he almost burst,
He thought it was not of the best.
Then cried he unto the child
To pipe no more within this place,
But to hold still for God's grace
And love of Mary Mild.

---

1 From this point onwards the text stops having strict six line stanzas.

Then said Jack to them each one,
'I will if you will promise me
To do me no villainy,
But let me go back home.'
Thereto they answered all anon.
And promised it would be all right,
And that they'd help in any fight
He'd have with anyone.

Thus they departed at that tide
From[1] the Official, the summoner,[2]
The stepdame, and the friar,
With great joy and much pride.

Thus endeth The Friar and the Boy.
Emprinted at London in Fleet Street at the sign of the Sun
by Wynkyn de Worde.

---

1 I have inserted 'from' to make the last four lines a better end to the poem. In the probable original version, everyone forgave and repented.   2 Bailiff of the Church court.

SCHOOL DAYS

It was only in the second half of the nineteenth century that free schooling for everyone was provided in Britain and North America. Before that, going to school depended on your parents thinking that it was worthwhile for you, being willing to do without your help or labour at home or in a farm or workshop, and being able to pay for your education. Many schools charged fees, and there were further expenses for writing materials, books, and so on.

We do not know how many children went to school in medieval Britain. It was certainly not everyone but it was, equally certainly, tens of thousands at any one time. Roughly speaking, there were two kinds of schools: reading and song schools on the one hand, and grammar schools on the other.

The reading and song schools were the more common and were attended by most children. It does not require much equipment or knowledge to teach a child to read. The task could be done by parents at home, if they were literate, especially by mothers. A fourteenth-century poem comparing the activities of men and of women includes the line 'Woman teacheth child on book'. There were many little schools teaching reading and charging small fees for doing so. Some were kept in private houses by women for girls and small boys, or by men for boys. Others were taught by clergy in churches.

At a school of this kind, boys and girls of the wealthier classes learnt how to read the Latin alphabet and pronounce simple Latin prayers. In the case of some schools for boys, song was also taught, meaning the ability to sing Latin words to plainsong. Having learnt to read and pronounce Latin words, it was not difficult to use your knowledge to read English, and most girls and many boys never got beyond that level.

Grammar schools were more ambitious. They were for boys alone and taught the full understanding of Latin: its grammar (word forms and meanings) and syntax (how to compose sentences). Boys learnt to write both Latin prose and verse, read Latin poetry, and studied linguistics: why language works as it does. Most boys even from grammar schools gave up such studies in their mid teens and entered everyday life and employment. Only a few went on to professions such as the Church and the law, where an advanced knowledge of Latin was needed.

Medieval schools, especially the grammar schools, have left many records of their activities, so that is possible to reconstruct the school day, the subjects that were studied, the discipline, and even the thoughts of the teachers and pupils in the class.

THE VALUE OF GOING TO SCHOOL

This maxim was written in Latin in the hall of a monastery in Cornwall, where local students were provided with meals:

It is good, while you are young, Learning's house to fare to;
They are foolish people who neither know nor care to.

LEARNING THE ABC

The first thing learnt at school was the alphabet, which was laid out and recited like a prayer. You began by crossing yourself and saying 'Christ's cross be my speed', or 'God speed me', or 'God help'. Then you pronounced the letters from A to Z. After Z, you said the shorthand signs for et (Latin for 'and'), con-, and the tittles or dots that stood for est (Latin for 'is'). Then you ended the prayer by saying 'Amen':

Christ's cross be my speed,
In all virtue to proceed.

> A B C D E F G
> H I K L M N O P
> Q R ST, U X Y Z
> And per se,
> Con per se,
> Tittle tittle, est. Amen.

Here are two pupils struggling to learn the alphabet, in a scene from a fifteenth-century play in Cornish from Camborne in Cornwall. The joke is that 'est' is the last word of the alphabet. You need only to say 'amen' afterwards:

> First Pupil God help! A, B, C,
>   After that comes D.
> That's my total, sadly.
> Second pupil E-S-T spells est;
>   I don't know what's next;
> Do not beat me badly!
>   I can go no higher;
>   Breakfast I require,
> Then I'll learn more gladly.

When John Trevisa set out to translate into English the large Latin encyclopaedia called On the Properties of Things, *his mind went back to his early schooldays, when he used to cross himself and say the alphabet. So he prayed to Christ in a similar way to help him with his task, which he finished in 1389:*

A cross was made of red
At the beginning of my book,
That is called 'God me speed',
In the first lesson that I took.

Then I learnèd A and B,
And other letters by their names,
But always 'God speed me'
Needful to me in all games.

If I played in fields or meads,
Either still or else with noise,
I prayed help in all my deeds
From Him who died upon the cross.

Now all my playings, in his name
I shall let pass forth and fare,
And try to play a longer game,
Also and I shall forswear

Woods, meads, and fields,
Places that I have played in,
And in His name, that all things wields,
This game now I shall begin,

And pray help, counsel, and rede[1]
That He them to me shall send,
And this game rule and lead
And bring it to a good end.

---

1 Advice.

READING AND SONG

After learning the alphabet, you practised reading words from a primer, a book of simple Latin prayers, beginning with the Paternoster. *When you could pronounce Latin properly, if you were a boy, you learnt to sing it in plainsong. The books commonly used for teaching reading and singing were the psalter (the 150 psalms) and the antiphonal (texts sung during Church services).*

At the end of the fourteenth century, Chaucer described a school that taught reading and song to small boys in his 'Prioress's Tale'. The hero of the tale, a child of seven, is studying the primer. His friend, an older boy, is learning to sing from the antiphonal, including the hymn Alma Redemptoris Mater, *in honour of the Virgin Mary. Neither boy yet knew fully 'grammar', in other words the meaning of the Latin that they were learning:*

A little school of Christian folk there stood
At the street's further end, in which there were
Children a-heap, all born of Christian blood,
Who learnt inside the school from year to year
The lore belonging to the people there:
To read and know how plainsong should be sung,
As little children do when they are young.

Among these children was a widow's lad,
A little clerkling of the age of seven.
Each day he went to school great joy he had
To pass a statue of Our Lady, given
In honour of the gentle Queen of Heaven,
And, as he had been taught, he knelt to say
Ave Maria[1] when he passed that way.

Thus did the widow teach her little son
To worship Mary, Christ's own mother dear,

---

1 Hail Mary.

And he this worship never left undone,
For children quickly learn the things they hear,
And I recall a saint I much revere,
St Nicholas, whose praise be ever sung:
For he too venerated Christ when young.

One day this little boy who sat among
The lowest pupils with their primers all,
Heard *Alma Redemptoris*[1] being sung
By children learning the antiphonal,
And daringly he drew himself so near
That he could follow as they sang it through,
Until the words of the first verse he knew.

He knew not what the Latin signified
Because he was so little and so young,
Until one day he to a friend applied
To know its meaning in his mother tongue
And to hear from him why the song was sung.
To have this knowledge he made many pleas
And even knelt to do so on bare knees.

His friend, who somewhat older was than he,
Answered him thus: 'This song, I have heard say,
Was made about our Blessed Lady, she
To whom we should do reverence and pray
For help when death takes us from life away.
But if I tell you more, it may be wrong:
I yet know little Latin, only song.'

'And is this song', replied the little boy,
'In praise of Christ's own mother? Then I vow
That all the time I have I will employ
To learn it through by Christmas, and although

---

1 Gracious [Mother] of the Redeemer.

I may neglect my primer, which I know
Will get me birched and birched, I will not vary
From honouring the Blessed Virgin Mary.'

And so his friend rehearsed him privately
From day to day until he knew by rote
The hymn, and sang it well and fearlessly
With every word according to its note.
Then twice a day it carolled from his throat:
Once going to school and once when home he went,
So set on Mary's praise was his intent.

LATIN GRAMMAR

*When you could read and sing Latin, you learnt the grammar of
the language in a grammar school. Grammar included the forms
of the words (Latin words have far more than do English ones),
their meanings, and how to put them together into sentences.
Some of the textbooks used in grammar schools were in verse,
because this made it easy to remember them. The next extract
is from one of the most popular Latin grammars, the* Doctrinale
*by Alexander of Ville-Dieu (written in about 1200). In it the pupil
learns the forms of Latin words of the first declension, such as*
mensa *('a table') and names like* Aeneas, Anchises, *and* Adam:

First declension nouns have -*as*, -*es*, -*a* for their endings,
As well as -*am* in some proper names taken from Hebrew.
Genitives, likewise datives, diphthongs carry in -*a-e*,
While the accusative gives us -*am*, although we discover
That -*es* and -*as* produce -*en* and -*an*, while all Greek words
Ending with -*a* become -*an* in a similar manner.
-*a* is the vocative form, but -*es* has an -*e* termination;
Ablatives also adopt -*a*, -*es* taking -*e* as beforehand,
Saving that -*am* in the first case stays so in both of the latter.

You also learnt Latin vocabulary: what words meant and what other words they were derived from. The lines that follow are translated from another widely-read grammar in Latin verse called the Grecismus *by Evrard of Béthune, a writer contemporary with Alexander of Ville-Dieu:*

An orátor is pupil under a rhetor's direction;
Rhetor from *resis* is taken; *oro* gives us the other.
Aër is air we breathe, *aether* that which is higher;
He who plays host is a *hospes*, so is the guest whom
   he welcomes,
Just as both carer and cared for merit the title *alumnus*;
One who composes in metre, him we entitle *poëta*,
One telling people their fortunes, him we refer to as *vates*,
While a *propheta* utters (Latin *profatur*) what's godly.

When you knew enough Latin words and their meanings, you were made to compose Latin, beginning with short sentences and going on to longer pieces of prose and even the writing of verse. English proverbs were sometimes used as practice for writing Latin; some of these were in rhyme and might themselves be translated into Latin verse:

Short horse soon wiped, little food soon fliped.[1]
   Curtus equus sito strigillatur, et modicus sibus illico liguritur.

Was he never good swain that stopped his errand for the rain.
   Quem retinet stille, non est bonus armiger ille.

Pepper is black but has a good smack.
   Piper est grossum, sed habet bonum preciosum.

At Easter nothing is so the way as eggs and alleluia!
   Ad festum pasche nihil ita vsuale, sicut oua et vox alleluia.

---

1 Gobbled up.

Be the summer day never so long, at last cometh evensong.
> Quam longa fuerit dies estiualis, tandem venit nox et vespere.

When the foot warmeth, the shoe harmeth.
> Calcius arescit quum pes igne calescit.

Winter eateth what summer getteth.
> Brume tempestas vorat hoc quod procreat estas.

It is merry in hall when beards wag all.
> Aula gaudescit cum barbula queque movescit.

When the game is best, it is time to rest.
> Cum melior iocus est, ipsum dimittere prodest.

When Adam delved and Eve span,[1]
Who was then a gentleman?
> Cum vanga quadam tellurem foderat Adam,
> Ac Eve nens fuerat, quis generosus erat?

When bloweth the broom, then wooeth the groom;
When bloweth the furze, then shall he woo worse.[2]
> Rusticus equestis procus est, florente murica;
> Rusco florente, nulla gaudebit amica.

He that hath an evil bill,[3] and goeth to the wood with evil will,
And himself be a shrew,[4] little wood he will hew.
> Pertusum restans falcastrum per nemus arrans,
> Prauus si fuerit lignicula pauca dolabit.

LATIN POETRY

Grammar-school boys studied Latin poetry just as we do Shakespeare or Wordsworth. One of the most commonly read poems

---

1 Spun wool.   2 Presumably: it is easier to woo in spring than summer.   3 A substandard bill-hook.   4 Villain.

was the Distichs of Cato, *a series of wise couplets dating from later Roman times. These are the first seven of them:*

Given that God is a spirit, which is what poetry tells us,
See that you offer him worship spiritually and purely.

Fix your devotion on keeping vigils rather than slumbers:
Resting during the daytime easily nourishes vices.

What is the first of the virtues? Guarding your tongue
    is the answer:
Those who pay honour to silence come very close to
    their Maker.

Try to avoid being either contrary or inconsistent;
He who disputes with himself surely will benefit no one.

If you consider men's actions, and in particular morals,
Reflect when folk lay blame: no one is free of offences.

What you possess that is harmful, though it is treasured,
    relinquish;
Usefulness rather than riches matters on any occasion.

As situations dictate, choose between mercy and firmness;
That should be thought of as wisdom rather than held a
    shortcoming.

Apart from Cato, classical Latin literature was little read in grammar schools between about 1200 and 1500. Instead, its place was taken by medieval Latin religious and moral poems. One of these was Stans Puer ad Mensam, *translated in the section on Manners. Here are three others. First,* The Eclogue of Theodulus, *a dialogue in which a shepherd and a shepherdess compare some of the chief stories of classical mythology with those of Biblical history. The message is that only the Bible is truthful. These are a few translated verses:*

Shepherd: First in the world came Saturn, out of the shores
   of the Cretans,
Sowing the human races over lands that were golden.
No one is named as his parent, no one existed before him;
All who are noble rejoice, having this god as their father.

Shepherdess: Man at his first creation lived in a paradise garden,
Till at his wife's persuasion, poisonous serpentine venom,
Which he consented in sharing, brought humanity's
   downfall;
Still their children suffer from their parents' transgression.

Shepherd: Jupiter being impatient, wishing to capture those
   riches,
Ousted his father Saturn, brutally taking up weapons.
Then, though the world grew paler, gold transmuting to silver,
King of the gods he became, ruling the palace of heaven.

Shepherdess: Adam was also ejected, cast from his God-given
   haven,
Changed from the model of nature into a being of ashes.
Those who would enter his garden, seeking the tree of
   the apple,
Meet with a terror to stop them: a sword burning and blazing.

Next, the Parallels *of Alain de Lille, a poet of France who died
in 1203. Each Latin verse evokes an image and then draws an
analogy from it. These are some of the opening lines, including a
waspish attack on women:*

Phoebe, the moon, acquires lustre from Phoebus the sun god;
So does a fool from a wise man, sparkling with light that is
   borrowed.

Etna, for all that she blazes, merely consumes her own
   substance,
Just as the fires of the jealous injure themselves but no others.

Even a pig on a dunghill rises in order to forage;
Why then do humans in contrast never forsake what is filthy?

What could be more of a folly: using a sieve to hold syrup?
So is imparting a secret into the mouth of a gossip.

Paths that are recent, not rooted, serve to deceive the wayfarer;
So with one's friendships: the new, not the well-tried and
    well-tested.

Nothing exists in a mirror, even though visible in it;
Such is the faith of a woman: specious, and yet an illusion.

Out of the tiniest granules grows the most mighty of horses;
Little sins generate likewise evil that may not be pardoned.

Lastly, the poem Cartula *('a little charter'). This is a gloomy account
of the transience of worldly things, relieved by an ornate style with an
internal rhyme in every line. The following translation is a sample:*

All that with beauty refreshes, everything that is precious,
Closely resembles a flower, coloured by natural power.
Soon it is fated to wither, passing whoever knows whither:
Empty, the place it embellished; vanished, the fragrance
    we relished.
Royalty too and its story, pomp and terrestrial glory,
All of the goods that we treasure, lives of whatever their measure,
Steadily move to an ending; death is for each of us pending;
Though its arrival is hidden, yet to its stroke we are bidden.
Hear then what constitutes glory: what need I write of its story?
It is enough that I tell you: nothing whatever has value.
Landed estates that are spacious, riches however capacious,
Frontages grandly enclosing mansions with features imposing,
Tables of succulent dishes formed to meet everyone's wishes,
Even the marriage bed's pleasures, chalices, cups, and such
    treasures,
Clothes of the fashion indecent that has found favour of recent,

Hundreds of cattle in keeping, acres of crops for the reaping,
Vineyards of grapes for our liquor, rich and replete for
   the picker,
Even your children, your foremost, even the One you
   adore most,
Must be relinquished for ever; you will recover them never.
What prudent person would trouble with such a brief
   flying bubble?
Death – let there be no illusion – brings us a bitter conclusion,
Once and for all superseding things so unsound and misleading.

DISCIPLINE

*Discipline in medieval schools was harsh by modern standards.
Even Chaucer's seven year-old boy expected to get beaten. In
this song (a carol, in fact, with a chorus sung after every verse),
a schoolboy complains about having to go school, arriving late,
and being birched on his bottom by the schoolmaster as a
punishment.*

Hey, hey, by this day,
What availeth it me though I say nay?

I would fain be a clerk,
But yet it is a strange work;
The birchen twigs be so sharp
It maketh me have a faint heart:
What availeth it me though I say nay?

On Monday in the morning when I shall rise,
At six of the clock, it is the guise
To go to school without avise:[1]

---

1 Without thinking about it.

I had rather go twenty mile twice.
 What availeth it me though I say nay?

My master looketh as he were mad:
'Where hast thou been, thou sorry lad?'
'Milking ducks[1] – my mother bade';
It were no marvel that I were sad:
 What availeth it me though I say nay?

My master peppered my arse with good speed;
It stung worse than fennel seed;
He would not leave till it did bleed:
Much sorrow have he for his deed!
 What availeth it me though I say nay?

I would my master were a Wat,[2]
And my book a wild cat,
And a brace of greyhounds in his top;
I would be glad for to see that.
 What availeth it me though I say nay?

I would my master were a hare,
And all his books hounds were,
And I myself a jolly hunter,
To blow my horn I would not spare,
For if he were dead I would not care:
 What availeth it me though I say nay?

Or as another pupil put it more concisely,

One more than three and fewer than five,
I had upon my bottom strokes full rife.

---

1 A saucy reply! 2 Hare.

THE END OF TERM

But schooling did not last throughout the year. There were occasional holidays on major saints' days and longer ones at Christmas, Easter, and in the summer, just as there are today. This is a poem for the last day of term before Christmas, partly in Latin and partly in English. It starts with the boys marching through the schoolroom up to the schoolmaster's chair:

Now that term is finishing, we've a stick to carry,
And the usher's[1] head with it, we shall hit and harry!
If the master questions us, whither we are going,
Briefly we'll reply to him, 'That's not for your knowing!'

Then the leader of the boys says to the master,

O most noble teacher, all of us pray
That you will grant and give us leave to play,
For now we intend, although you say 'no',
To break up from school, I tell you that's so.
The feast that approaches is for joy, we conceive,
So today we have chosen to take our leave.
After Christmas full sore shall we quake
When we return, Latin proses to make,
But now we ask heartily, each one and all,
That today we be allowed to break up from school.

So they all go home, and this book breaks up too!

GOODBYE!

---

1 The usher was the schoolmaster's assistant.

FURTHER READING

Nicholas Orme, *Medieval Children* (New Haven and London, Yale University Press, 2001), and *Medieval Schools* (New Haven and London, Yale University Press, 2006), include detailed accounts of childhood, youth, and schooling in medieval England.

Helen Cooper, *Great Grandmother Goose* (London, Hamish Hamilton, 1978) is a pioneer collection of modernised, short, medieval rhymes similar in character to later nursery rhymes.

Nicholas Orme, *Early School Exercises* (Toronto, Institute of Pontifical Studies, forthcoming 2012–13) will edit the major collections of Latin and English sentences in school exercise books, which include several of the rhymes in the present collection.

Julia Boffey and A. S. G. Edwards, *A New Index of Middle English Verse* (London, British Library, 2006) is the standard list of such texts in verse with information about the manuscripts in which they are found and the modern editions of them. This is coded *NIMEV* in the notes that follow.

NOTES

1. GROWING UP

p. 9. When a woman's time is near. Mid 13th century. Author's translation
from Walter of Bibbesworth, *Le Tretiz*, ed. W. Rothwell, Anglo-Norman
Text Society, Plain Texts Series, 6 (1990), p. 3.

p. 9. The food that you lay. Early 14th century. Robert Mannyng, *Handlyng
Synne*, ed. Idelle Sullens (Binghampton, NY, 1983), lines 9675–80.

p. 10. This yonder night. 15th century. NIMEV, 3628. *Religious Lyrics of the
XVth Century*, ed. Carleton Brown (Oxford, 1939), p. 7.

p. 10. Watch well, Annot. 14th century. NIMEV, 3859.5. *Secular Lyrics of the XIVth
and XVth Centuries*, ed. R. H. Robbins, 2nd ed. (Oxford, 1955), p. xxxix.

p. 11. Put your clothes on. Author's translation from Walter of Bibbesworth, p. 6.

p. 11. If your toddler. Author's translation from ibid., p. 7.

p. 12. I have twelve oxen. Early 16th century. NIMEV, 1314. *Secular Lyrics*, ed. Robbins, p. 42. This song is from a manuscript anthology of
poems made by Richard Hill, a London merchant, but one that shows
signs of being meant for family as well as personal use, so that the
song could have been sung to his children.

p. 12. Tom-a-lin and his wife. 16th-century record. William Wager, *The
Longer Thou Livest the More Fool Thou Art*, (1569), ed. R. Mark Benbow (London, 1968), p. 7.

p. 13. The hare went to market. 15th century, from a (mainly) school
miscellany. NIMEV, 3372.5. S. B. Meech, 'A Collection of Proverbs in
Rawlinson MS D 328', *Modern Philology*, 38 (1940–1), p. 124.

p. 13. Hares and foxes. 15th century, from a school miscellany. NIMEV,
1089.55. David Thomson, *A Descriptive Catalogue of Middle English Grammati-
cal Texts* (New York and London, 1979), p. 146.

p. 13. The cricket and the grasshopper. 15th century, from a school miscellany. NIMEV, 3324. *Secular Lyrics*, ed. Robbins, p. 104.

p. 13.The owl to the stone. 15th century, from a (mainly) school miscel-lany. Meech, 'A Collection of Proverbs', p. 120.

p. 14. The gentle broom on hive hill. Mid 16th century. This and the songs that follow come from Wager, *The Longer Thou Livest*, ed. Benbow, pp. 7–8 (compare also pp. 39–40).

p. 15. At my house I have a jay. 15th-century school exercise. *NIMEV*, 430.8. C. E. Wright, 'Late Middle English Parerga in a School Collec-tion', *Review of English Studies*, new series 2 (1951), pp. 114–20.

p. 15. If I were as swift as a swallow. 15th-century school exercise. Author's reconstruction of English from Latin translation. *The Winchester Anthology: a facsimile of British Library Additional Manuscript 60577*, ed. Edward Wilson (Cambridge, 1981), f. 75r.

p. 15. Five herrings for a penny. 15th-century school exercise. British Library, Harley MS 1587, f. 105r.

p. 16. We are three. 15th-century school exercise. Author's reconstruc-tion of English from Latin translation. *The Winchester Anthology*, ed. Wil-son, f. 75v.

p. 16. The miller's daughter. 15th-century school exercise. Author's reconstruction of English from Latin translation. Ibid., f. 74v.

p. 16. It happened on a certain day. 15th century; other versions exist back to the early 14th. *NIMEV*, 250. *Sammlung Altenglischer Legenden*, ed. C. Horstmann (Heilbronn, 1878), p. 106.

p. 18.The second age, I understand. *NIMEV*, 2235. 15th century work by (forename unknown) Rait, *Ratis Raving*, ed. J. R. Lumby, Early English Text Society, original series, 43 (1870), pp. 57–8.

p. 18. Now at the mark. Ibid., pp. 60–1.

p. 19. Each time and season. 1510s. Alexander Barclay, *The Eclogues of Alex-ander Barclay*, ed. Beatrice White, Early English Text Society, original series, 175 (1928), p. 184.

p. 19. Cockerel denominated. 15th-century school miscellany. Author's translation from Latin, Cambridge, St John's College, MS F.26, ff. 28v-29r. I have omitted an unpleasant second verse.

p. 20. Pancakes I gladly will taste. 1478, noted by the scholar William Worcester apparently while visiting Launceston in Cornwall, in a group of notes that seem to have come from a school manuscript.The translation is by John Harvey. William Worcester, *Itineraries*, ed. J. H. Harvey (Oxford, 1969), pp. 82–3.

p. 20. I have not eaten half my fill. 15th-century school exercise. Orme, *Education and Society*, p. 112.

p. 20. Let us now rejoice together. 11th century. Author's translation from *Analecta Hymnica Medii Aevi*, ed. G. M. Dreves, C. Blume, and H. N. Bannister, vol. 54 (Leipzig, 1915), pp. 95–6.

p. 22. For bread. E. K. Chambers, *The Medieval Stage*, 2 vols (Oxford, 1948), p. 288.

p. 22. Make we merry, both more and less. Early 16th century. *NIMEV*, 1866. *The Early English Carols*, ed. R. L. Greene, 2nd ed (Oxford, 1977), p. 6. This is another item from Richard Hill's anthology.

p. 23. Both man and child. Late 15th century. *NIMEV*, 67. *Early English Carols*, ed. Greene, p. 37.

p. 24. We pray for the lord. Early 15th century. Oxford, Bodleian Library, MS Lincoln College lat. 130, f. 1r.

2. WORDS, RHYMES, AND SONGS

p. 27. Children are soft of flesh. 1389. John Trevisa's English translation of the 13th-century Latin work by Bartholomew the Englishman, *De Proprietatibus Rerum. On the Properties of Things*, ed. M. C. Seymour and others, 3 vols (Oxford, 1975–88), i, 300–1.

p. 27. How many miles. 13th century. Quoted in a Latin sermon, partly in Latin, partly English, the latter listed in *NIMEV*, 0.3. Oxford, Balliol College, MS 230, f. 153v.

p. 28. Three grey greedy geese. 15th-century school exercise. Nicholas Orme, *Education and Society in Medieval and Renaissance England* (London, 1989), p. 84.

p. 28. Fleas, flies, and friars. 15th-century school miscellany. British Library, Harley MS 3362, f. 24r *NIMEV*, 808.

p. 29. Three headless men. *NIMEV*, 1354. 15th century, from a (mainly) school miscellany. Meech, 'Collection of Proverbs', p. 125. Also in another manuscript and (as seven men) in Latin in a school exercise in *The Winchester Anthology*, ed. Wilson, f. 75r.

p. 30. Bloodless and boneless. 15th-century school exercise. Orme, *Education and Society*, p. 100.

p. 30. Will you hear a wondrous thing. 15th century. *NIMEV*, 4169. *The English and Scottish Popular Ballads*, ed. F. J. Child, 5 vols (New York, 1967), v, 283–4. The source is a 15th-century manuscript belonging to Walter Pollard of Exeter and Plymouth. Some of its contents relate to his school days, others to his later life, so we cannot be sure at what age he copied this down (Thomson, *A Descriptive Catalogue*, pp. 290–315).

p. 30. In dock, out nettle. 15th-century school exercise. British Library, Harley MS 1587, f. 104v. There was more of the saying than this, because the words end 'etc.' Longer versions are found in later times, e.g. 'Nettle in, dock out; dock rub nettle out'.

p. 30 Mark, Matthew, Luke, and John. The first line occurs in a 15th-century courtesy book. *Early English Meals and Manners*, ed. F. J. Furnivall, Early English Text Society, original series, 32 (1868, repr. 1931), p. 181. The second line comes from the next oldest record of the rhyme in 1656 (but allegedly dating back to the mid 16th century), and there are later longer versions. *The Oxford Dictionary of Nursery Rhymes*, ed. Iona and Peter Opie, 2nd ed. (Oxford, 1997), pp. 357–60.

p. 31. If it so betide. 15th-century school exercise. *The Winchester Anthology*, ed. Wilson, f. 76r.

p. 31. Who steals this book. 15th-century school manuscript. Author's translation from Latin. Thomson, *A Descriptive Catalogue*, p. 292.

p. 31. By street or way. *NIMEV*, 4152. 15th-century courtesy book. *Early English Meals and Manners*, ed. Furnivall, p. 187.

p. 31. I saw a sparrow. 15th-century school exercise. Orme, *Education and Society*, p. 102.

p. 31. At harvest time. 15th-century school exercise. Wright, 'Late Middle English Parerga', pp. 239–53.

p. 32. I saw three snails. 15th-century school exercise. Author's reconstruction of English from Latin translation. *The Winchester Anthology*, ed. Wilson, f. 75r.

p. 32. Hey, hey, hey, hey. *NIMEV*, 1350. Early 16th century. *Early English Carols*, ed. Greene, pp. 289–90. A further item from Richard Hill's collection.

p. 33. Hur! Hur! 15th-century school exercise. British Library, Harley MS 1587, f. 104r.

p. 33. John, John. 15th century, from a (mainly) school miscellany. Meech, 'A Collection of Proverbs', p. 119.

p. 34. I will have the whip. Late 15th- or early 16th-century school exercise, the first phrase in English, the rest the author's reconstruction from Latin translation. Orme, *Education and Society*, p. 119.

p. 34. Thou stinkest, etc. Early 16th-century school text. *The Vulgaria of John Stanbridge and . . . Robert Whittinton*, ed. Beatrice White, Early English Text Society, original series, 187 (1932), pp. 17–20.

p. 34. A fox and a polecat. *NIMEV*, 35.5. 15th-century school exercise. *The Winchester Anthology*, ed. Wilson, f. 76v; also in another manuscript.

p. 35. Souters have an extravagant pride. 15th-century school exercise. Ibid., f. 76r.

p. 35. Harry Hotspur. 15th century. *NIMEV*, 1185. This is not in a manuscript associated with youth, but it looks youthful and harmonises with the next two pieces in this anthology.

p. 35. Hairy Scot in a raveling. 15th-century school exercise. Orme, *Education and Society*, p. 82.

p. 36. Martin Swart and his man. Composed in about 1487; 16th-century record. Wager, *The Longer Thou Livest*, ed. Benbow, p. 7.

p. 36. Underneath a louver. 15th-century school exercise. *The Winchester Anthology*, ed. Wilson, f. 76v.

p. 36. Flowers in my arbour. 15th-century school exercise. Ibid., f. 76v.

p. 36. At stone throwing. Two slight different versions, late 12th and 13th centuries. *NIMEV*, 445. *Secular Lyrics*, ed. Robbins, p. xxxix.

p. 37. O Robin, I will marry you. 15th-century school exercise. *The Winchester Anthology*, ed. Wilson, f. 75r.

p. 37. Wed me, Robin. 15th-century school exercise. Ibid., f. 76r.

p. 37. Alas! alas! the while. 15th century. *NIMEV*, 1849. *Early English Carols*, ed. Greene, pp. 276–7 (other similar carols are printed on pp. 275–9). I have included this on the grounds that it relates to a teenage girl, and because there is other prose evidence about knowledge of sex by children.

3. MANNERS MAKETH MAN

p. 40. Rax and wax. 15th-century school exercise. *The Winchester Anthology*, ed. Wilson, f. 76v.

p. 41. When thou art in Rome. 15th century, from a (mainly) school miscellany. Meech, 'Collection of Proverbs', p. 122.

p. 41. When I lent I had a friend. 15th century, from the same miscellany. Bodleian Library, MS Rawlinson D 328, f. 168r.

p. 41. Arise early. 15th-century. *NIMEV*, 324. Several versions; this one is from *Stans Puer ad Mensam* (London, William Caxton, 1476). Author's modernisation in John Lydgate, *Table Manners for Children* (Salisbury, Perdix Press, 1989; repr. London, Wynkyn de Worde Society, 1990), p. 30.

p. 41. My dearest child. *NIMEV*, 2233. *Stans Puer ad Mensam*, translated by John Lydgate, died *c*.1451. From the same edition of *Stans Puer Ad Mensam*. Author's modernisation in the same edition as above, pp. 22–30.

p. 45. Afore all things. 15th-century. *NIMEV*, 1919. Author's modernisation from *Caxton's Book of Courtesy*, ed. F. J. Furnivall, Early English Text Society, extra series 3 (1868), pp. 4, 8–9.

p. 46. All who come to dinner. 15th-century. Author's translation, in Nicholas Orme, 'Castrianus: a fifteenth-century poem of school life', *Notes and Queries*, 255 (2010), pp. 484–90, from the Latin poem *Castrianus*, edited by M. R. James, 'Castrianus: an address to the Eton commensals of the fifteenth century', *Etoniana*, 39 (30 Nov 1925), pp. 609–14, and by Servus Gieben, 'Robert Grosseteste and Medieval Courtesy Books', *Vivarium*, 5 (1967), pp. 71–4.

p. 49. Daughter, if thou wilt. 14th-century. *NIMEV*, 671. *The Good Wife Taught her Daughter*, ed. T. F. Mustanoja (Helsinki, 1948), Text E, pp 158–70.

p. 54. Wheresoever you fare. 15th-century. *NIMEV*, 4064. *English Hunting and Hawking in The Boke of St Albans*, ed. Rachel Hands (Oxford, 1975), pp. 57–79, compared with pp. 168–86.

4. STORIES

p. 59. Lithe and listen. 15th century. *NIMEV*, 1915. From *A Lytell Gest of Robyn Hode* (London and other places, various editions from about 1500 onwards), modern edition in *Rymes of Robin Hood*, ed. R. B. Dobson and J. Taylor, 2nd ed. (Stroud, 1997), pp. 99–102.

p. 64. Our king he kept a false steward. 17th-century text that is probably a revision of something earlier than at least 1549. P. Christopherson, *The Ballad of Sir Aldingar: its origin and analogues* (Oxford, 1952), pp. 167–73.

p. 72. There dwelt a farmer. 15th century. *NIMEV*, 977. *The Frere and the Boy* (London, Wynkyn de Worde, 1510–13). There is another early 16th-century version of the text in Richard Hill's manuscript (E. Flügel, 'Liedersammlungen des XVI Jahrhunderts', part 3, *Anglia*, 26 (1903), pp. 105–32). It is neater than de Worde's, but I have printed his rougher version as being the one likely to have circulated most widely.

5. SCHOOL DAYS

p. 85 It is good while you are young. 15th-century. Author's translation of a Latin inscription formerly at Launceston Priory, Cornwall. Nicholas Orme, *Victoria History of the County of Cornwall*, vol. 2 (London, 2010), p. 207.

p. 86. Christ's cross be my speed. Several 15th- and 16th-century examples are listed in Orme, *Medieval Children*, p. 253.

p. 86. ABC. This is a conjectural reconstruction of the alphabet as a poem. Early presentations of the alphabet do not follow a consistent pattern, but it is likely that some rhythm was observed when reciting it. See Orme, *Medieval Children*, p. 60.

p. 86. God help! A, B, C. 15th-century play in Cornish, *Beunans Meriasek*, discussed in Nicholas Orme, "Education in the Cornish Play *Beunans Meriasek*', *Cambridge Medieval Celtic Studies*, 25 (1993), pp. 1–13. 'God help!' is another variant of 'Christ's cross be my speed.'

p. 87. A cross was made of red. NIMEV, 33. 1380s, by John Trevisa. *On the Properties of Things*, ed. Seymour and others, i, 40.

p. 88. A little school of Christian folk. Late 14th century. Author's modernisation of Geoffrey Chaucer, *The Riverside Chaucer*, ed. Larry D. Benson and others (Oxford, 1987), pp. 209–10 (VII. 495–550; B2 1685–1740). Chaucer wrote primarily for adults, but there are later references to children reading or being encouraged to read his work.

p. 90. First declension nouns. c.1200. Author's translation from Alexander of Ville-Dieu, *Das Doctrinale des Alexander de Villa Dei*, ed. D. Reichling (Berlin, 1893), p. 8 (lines 29–37).

p. 91. An *orátor* is pupil. c.1200. Author's translation from Evrard of Béthune, *Eberhardi Bethuniensis Graecismus*, ed. J. Wrobel (Breslau, 1887), p. 71.

p. 91. Short horse soon wiped. 15th-century school exercise. Orme, *Education and Society*, p. 100.

p. 91. Was he never good swain. 15th-century school exercise. Ibid., p. 83.

p. 91. Pepper is black. 15th-century school exercise. Ibid., p. 83.

p. 91. At Easter nothing is so the way. 15th-century school exercise. Ibid., p. 84.

p. 92. Be the summer day never so long. 15th-century school exercise. Ibid., p. 85.

p. 92. When the foot warmeth. 15th-century school exercise. British Library, Harley MS 1587, f. 105r.

p. 92. Winter eateth. 15th century, from a (mainly) school miscellany. Meech, 'Collection of Proverbs', p. 118.

p. 92. It is merry in hall. 15th century. Ibid., p. 120.

p. 92. When the game is best. 15th century. Ibid.

p. 92. When Adam delved. 15th century. Ibid., p. 121. The proverb was older, and was famously quoted in the Peasants' Revolt of 1381.

p. 92. When bloweth the broom. 15th-century school exercise. Ibid., f. 105v.

p. 92. He that hath an evil bill. 15th-century school exercise. *TheWinchester Anthology*, ed. Wilson, f. 76r.

p. 93. Given that God is a spirit. 3rd century. Author's translation from *Disticha Catonis*, ed. M. Boas and H. J. Botschuyver (Amsterdam, 1952), pp. 34–9.

p. 94. First in the world came Saturn. 10th century. Author's translation from *Theoduli Eclogam*, ed. J. Osternacher (Linz, 1902), pp. 32–3.

p. 94. Phoebe, the moon, acquires lustre. Late 12th century. Author's translation from J. P. Migne, *Patrologia Latina* (Paris, 1844–65), vol. 210, col. 581.

p. 95. All that with beauty refreshes. 12th or 13th century. Author's translation from ibid., vol. 184, cols 1307–14.

p. 96. Hey, hey, by this day. Early 16th-century text of probable 15th-century carol. *NIMEV*, 1399. *Early English Carols*, ed. Greene, pp. 245–6.

p. 97. One more than three. 15th-century school exercise. Orme, *Education and Society*, p. 111.

p. 98. Now that term is finishing. 15th century. Part Latin, part English. Author's translation from British Library, Sloane MS 1584, f. 33r, printed in *Reliquiae Antiquae*, ed. T. Wright and J. O. Halliwell, 2 vols (London, 1841–3), i, 116–17.

INDEX